The rapid growth of academic literature in the field of economics has posed serious problems for both students and teachers of the subject. The latter find it difficult to keep pace with more than a few areas of their subject, so that an inevitable trend towards specialism emerges. The student quickly loses perspective as the maze of theories and models grows and the discipline accommodates an increasing amount of quantitative techniques.

'Macmillan Studies in Economics' is a new series which sets out to provide the student with short, reasonably critical surveys of the developments within the various specialist areas of theoretical and applied economics. At the same time, the studies aim to form an integrated series so that, seen as a whole, they supply a balanced overview of the subject of economics. The emphasis in each study is upon recent work, but each topic will generally be placed in a historical context so that the reader may see the logical development of thought through time. Selected bibliographies are provided to guide readers to more extensive works. Each study aims at a brief treatment of the salient problems in order to avoid clouding the issues in detailed argument. Nonetheless, the texts are largely self-contained, and presume only that the student has some knowledge of elementary micro-economics and macro-economics.

Mathematical exposition has been adopted only where necessary. Some recent developments in economics are not readily comprehensible without some mathematics and statistics, and quantitative approaches also serve to shorten what would otherwise be lengthy and involved arguments. Where authors have found it necessary to introduce mathematical techniques, these techniques have been kept to a minimum. The emphasis is upon the economics, and not upon the quantitative methods. Later studies in the series will provide analyses of the links between quantitative methods, in particular econometrics, and economic analysis.

MACMILLAN STUDIES IN ECONOMICS

General Editors: D. C. ROWAN and G. R. FISHER

Executive Editor: D. W. PEARCE

Published

Forthcoming

Transport Economics

C. H. SHARP

Senior Lecturer in Economics, University of Leicester

Macmillan

First published 1973 by
THE MACMILLAN PRESS LTD
London and Basingstoke
Associated companies in New York Dublin
Melbourne Johannesburg and Madras

SBN 333 12626 2

Printed in Great Britain by
THE ANCHOR PRESS LTD
Tiptree, Essex

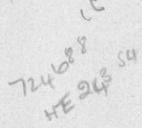

Contents

Acknowledgements

I should like to thank my colleagues, Tony Jennings and Michael Webb, for their help in reading the draft of this book and in discussing some of the issues with me. I should also like to thank Mrs Gay Best and Mrs J. Hirst for their skill and patience in interpreting my manuscript.

C.H.S.

1 The Basic Problems of Transport Economics

The study of transport economics involves undertaking the intriguing but often very difficult task of applying the methods of economic analysis to the complex and involved problems of the real world. In this real world it is not only the best means of obtaining objectives that have to be determined; the policy aims themselves may also be disputed, or changing, or unclear. Transport economics is an area in which the economist may find it very hard indeed to act as an independent and impartial expert who can discuss means without questioning ends. It is a field of study in which he will have to measure that which appears to be unmeasureable, and to deal not only with tangible scarce resources but also with more elusive items on which no market has ever bestowed a price. In order to resolve some transport problems it may be necessary to find a money value for such events or actions as spending another five minutes in bed in the morning, preserving a Norman church, having heavy lorries passing by the front room window or saving human life.

Although there may be special difficulties in finding solutions to some of the problems of transport economics, the problems themselves are basically the familiar ones of microeconomic analysis. The area in which the help of the transport economist is most often sought, and about which most has been written, is that of investment appraisal. The evaluation of transport investment can occur at all levels, from decisions on the proper share of total national investment that should be allocated to transport, to the economic investigation of a small-scale road improvement scheme. Discussion of the place of total transport investment in the economy, or of the allocation of transport investment between the different modes of transport, has been related mostly to developing or to highly centrally planned economies [54]. In developed, free-enterprise economies, like Britain and the United States, transport investment decisions are shared by so many different government bodies, companies and individuals, and the situation is so complex, that little has been written on global transport investment strategy. By far the greatest amount of attention has been given to the evaluation of individual investment projects, though these may sometimes be as large and important as the building of a national airport or the construction of a new underground railway ([22], [37]). Transport investment appraisal has been one of the most important areas in which attempts have been made to take account of social as well as private costs and returns, and in which techniques of cost–benefit analysis have been developed. The economic theory dealing with the choice between present and future satisfactions, and the discounting techniques based on this theory, also have an important place in the appraisal of investment in transport infrastructure [33].

The second major area of discussion in transport economics relates to the problem of resource allocation. This is, of course, closely related to investment issues. There are various reasons why the price mechanism may not be a wholly adequate means of allocating transport services, and why it may give misleading information to consumers. The widespread existence of joint costs in the provisions of transport services and the lack of a homogeneous unit of transport 'output' both mean that the relationship between price and cost may be uncertain and likely to vary. The problem of choosing between short-run marginal costs, long-run marginal costs and average costs as a suitable basis for charging is also very important ([36], [67]). Transport prices may be distorted by government taxes and subsidies, and by the difficulties of charging for the provision of infrastructure. Some government actions that affect the transport industry bear the implication that this is an area in which absolute consumer sovereignty may not be desirable. In particular, it has been suggested that people may not act wholly rationally in pricing the use of their own cars [62] and that transport managers in firms may not be efficient in allocating goods traffic [19].

With both the investment and pricing problems there are two issues that occur frequently, and that run through a great deal of the discussion of transport economics. The first of these is the place of government in an industry which, in Britain as almost everywhere else in the world, is partly in the public and partly in the private sector. The government is omnipresent in transport, either as a direct provider of services and of infrastructure, or as the source of the taxes, subsidies, and numerous regulations that affect the industry.

The second major factor that is important in dealing with the investment and pricing problems is the need to be able to measure the value of time. The main product of any transport investment is usually a reduction in journey or transit times. Information on the money value of time is therefore essential in transport investment appraisal, whether this relates to the location of the third London airport or to an urban road improvement. It is also of vital importance in appraising government decision on such issues as the fixing of speed limits and the introduction of minimum power-to-weight legislation for lorries.

There are a very considerable number of different forms of transport that could be considered in a survey of the problems of transport economics. These include road, rail, air, shipping, pipeline and inland waterways. Each of these main transport methods can be subdivided in various ways. There are underground, overhead and surface rail services, domestic and international air services, and coastal and international shipping lines. Road transport can be classified by the method of transportation used, the main ones being car, lorry, bicycle, bus and walking. There is also an important distinction between 'public transport', or buses, trains and general haulage lorries, which offer their services to all, and 'private transport', such as private cars, own-vehicle lorries and bicycles, which are used exclusively by their owners for their own transport purposes. Although much 'public transport' is also owned by public bodies such as local authorities and public corporations, the greater part of 'public' road haulage is operated by private firms. Cutting across all the other classifications of transport services is the very important distinction between goods and passenger transport, each of these having different economic problems. In order to keep this survey within reasonable length, only domestic transport will be discussed, and consideration of the problems of international air and shipping services has been excluded.

11

2 Transport Statistics

The quality of statistical information on domestic transport in Britain is uneven. Figures on all forms of rail transport and on road passenger transport are based on detailed annual returns and are relatively reliable (although some doubts have been expressed about the accuracy of the returns made by some bus undertakings). Figures on road goods transport and on private passenger transport are based on much less secure foundations [13]. Estimates of road goods traffic depend on sample surveys made by the Department of the Environment.[1] The last survey on which current information is based was carried out in 1968, though more recent data are just becoming available from a survey made in 1971. Figures based on these surveys contain two main possible sources of error. The Ministry surveys are samples, so that there is the chance of sampling errors, and figures in other years are based on possibly misleading projections of the sample data. A general difficulty of transport statistics is that there is no homogeneous unit of output that can be measured. The units most generally used are passenger miles and ton miles, but, as Bayliss and Hebden have demonstrated [24], these suffer from the disadvantage that they may not reflect accurately the resources used in different transport operations. The economic importance of air passenger transport relative to coach transport, for example, is underestimated if they are both measured in passenger miles, since the airlines consume extra resources to produce the superior product of quicker travel. Similarly, the resources used in 'own-vehicle' operation are underestimated by ton mileage figures since a large proportion of their work is in town areas with low average speeds. Expenditure figures would to some extent give a better picture of the resources used up if the effect of all taxes and

[1] References to the Department of the Environment should be taken as referring also to the Ministry of Transport, which existed until 1970. The Ministry of Transport Industries, which is now part of the Department of the Environment, continues most of the functions of the former Ministry.

subsidies were removed, but on the other hand taxes and subsidies may serve to 'correct' market prices to allow for social costs and benefits. The approximate importance of the main modes of transport in 1968, measured by ton miles and passenger miles, is shown in Table 1.

Table 1   The importance of main methods of transport in Great Britain, 1970

Transport method	Goods traffic 1970 Thousand million ton miles	%	Passenger traffic 1970 Thousand million passenger miles	%
Road – private	50·8	61·0	196·2	77·3
– public			34.1	13·4
Rail	16·4	19·7	22·2	8·8
Coastal shipping	14·2	17·0	–	–
Inland waterways	0·1	0·1	–	–
Pipelines	1·8	2·2	–	–
Air	–	–	1·2	0·5
	83·3	100·0	253·7	100·0

If the statistics of trends, rather than the figures for an individual year, are examined then two main points of interest emerge. In the last twenty years the volume of goods traffic carried by rail has declined (although there has been a slight reversal of the downward trend since 1967), while that carried by road has increased, and road has replaced rail as the most important carrier of freight traffic. In 1952 rail carried an estimated 22·4 thousand million ton miles while road carried 18·3 thousand million ton miles. Road and rail carried approximately equal tonnages in 1957, but by 1970 the position had become as shown in Table 1.

The other outstanding change in the distribution of traffic in recent years has been the growth of private road passenger traffic and the decline of public passenger transport. In the period from 1952 to 1968 the estimated total passenger miles of road public service vehicles declined from 50·1 to 36·3 thousand million, while estimated private road transport increased from 37·9 to 177·7 thousand million passenger miles. The public passenger decline has been almost entirely in carrying by stage buses, express coach services having retained a nearly constant passenger mileage. Estimated rail passenger mileage declined from 24·1 to 20·8 thousand million between 1952 and 1968, but increased again to 22·2 thousand million by 1970. Estimates of air passenger miles (which include flights to Northern Ireland and the Channel Isles as well as those within Great Britain) show a rapid growth from 0·1 thousand million in 1952 to 1·2 thousand million in 1968.

It is far from easy to obtain an accurate estimate of how much of the total national income is spent on transport. The National Income and Expenditure 'Blue Book' contains estimates of personal expenditure on transport, but it does not separate out the expenditure of industry on vehicles used for carrying its own goods, nor does it provide figures of depreciation costs. Gwilliam [39] quotes United Nations statistics, which estimated that 7·7 per cent of the total U.K. labour force was employed in transport and communications in 1962. Dawson [32] has calculated that the total net expenditure on road transport in Great Britain in 1966 was £4520 million. This figure represents actual resources used, since taxes and depreciation costs were deducted, and an allowance was made for double counting. The total national income of the United Kingdom in 1966 was £30,174 million. Since Northern Ireland was included in the national income figure but excluded from the transport expenditure estimate, it can be concluded that expenditure on road transport alone in 1966 constituted rather more than 15·0 per cent of the national income. In 1969 (when the national income was £35,354 million and G.D.P. was £38,576 million) the total expenditure of British Railways on operation, interest charges and gross investment amounted to £606·6 million. According to the Family Expenditure Survey figures, expenditure of the average household on 'transport and vehicles' in 1969 amounted to 13·9 per cent of total household expenditure. This compared with 26·1 per cent on food and 12·4 per cent on housing, the two other largest items in the family budget. Alternative estimates for consumers' expenditure on transport (based on the National Income and Expenditure figures and contained in Highway Statistics) as a percentage of all consumer expenditure were 9·5 per cent in 1969 and 9·9 per cent in 1970. The allocation of the estimated 1970 consumers' expenditure was: buses and coaches, £439 million; cars and motor cycles, £2649 million; rail, £232 million; sea and air, £290 million.

3 Transport Investment

In analysing the way in which transport investment is carried out it is necessary not only to consider the techniques of decision-making, but also to examine who it is that takes the investment decisions. In Britain the government, public corporations, local authorities, companies and private individuals all make or influence transport investment decisions.

The British Railways Board is the investment decision-making body for the railways in so far as it can draw up plans for the investment that it would like to take place. It is, however, almost wholly dependent on the government for the capital to finance its investment plans, so that they can be implemented only if the government is convinced of their desirability. This means that the government (which may mean the Minister for Transport Industries, or the Secretary for the Environment, or the Treasury, or the Cabinet) is now the ultimate decision-maker for all rail transport investment.

Like other public corporations, the Railways Board is not allowed to raise capital direct from the public, and would probably find it difficult to float loan issues on the market even if it had the freedom to do so. Investment could, of course, be financed from profits, but until 1969 the railways had not made a net surplus since 1952 [23]. The 1969 surplus of £14·7 million was achieved only after a capital debt had been reduced (under the 1968 Transport Act) from £1252 million to £365 million, and government grants of £76 million had been added into the revenue accounts as part of gross income.

Decisions on investment in roads are made by the government and by local authorities, but with the main decision firmly in the hands of the central government. The Department of the Environment pays the whole of the cost of investment in motorways and trunk roads, and 75 per cent of the cost of building principal roads (which are equivalent to trunk roads inside the areas of county borough councils). The improvement of minor roads is also partly paid for by the central government through the Rate Support Grant, which is a general grant to local authorities. The size of this grant is determined, amongst other things, by the mileage of road in the local authority area. Investment in road goods vehicles is made by the decision of a large number of road haulage undertakings (which range in size from large companies with several thousand vehicles to one-man, one-vehicle concerns), by the former 'C' licence operators who run vehicles to carry their own goods and by the publicly owned National Freight Corporation. The N.F.C. now controls British Road Services (General Haulage, Contract and Parcels) and the former parcels and small consignments (consignments in the weight range 28 pounds to 3 tons) carrying road fleet of British Railways. In all, in 1969 the National Freight Corporation owned about 24,000 vehicles [20].

The bus industry, and bus investment decision, is now almost wholly within the public sector. Buses are operated either by local authorities, by passenger transport authorities or by the nationalised National Bus Company. If investment is defined as the purchase of capital goods that are used to produce final consumption goods, then it could be argued that buying a motor-car is not an investment. But cars perform exactly the same service of moving people around as do buses or passenger trains, and the purchase of cars must be considered as an essential part of the total picture of transport investment. The car purchase investment decision is made partly by firms, but mostly, of course, by individuals. Finally, investment in ancillary road 'plant', which includes road-building machinery, garages and petrol stations, is made by private industry.

Port and dock investment decisions in Britain are made both by private companies and by public bodies. Ports may be owned by companies, by local authorities, or by special semi-public undertakings like the Port of London Authority. The docks at twenty ports (the largest being Southampton, Grimsby and Hull) are owned by the British Transport Docks Board [12]. The government can control major local authority investment through its power of loan sanction, and may control private development by the use of its planning powers. Investment in coastal shipping is made mainly by private industry, though British Railways and the National Freight Corporation have shipping interests. (It is planned to give control of the two N.F.C. shipping lines to British Railways.) Pipeline investment

16

is carried out by private industry, so far mainly by oil companies wishing to carry their own products. The construction of pipelines is controlled by the Pipe-Lines Act of 1962 [39]. Investment in inland waterways is made by the British Waterways Board and is mainly financed by loans from the government.

Investment decisions relating to airports are also made partly in the public and partly in the private sector, but in this case the public sector decisions are by far the most important. The major airports are operated by the British Airports Authority and investment decisions are effectively controlled by the central government.

Part of the difficulty of making correct transport investment decisions arises from the existence of these different forms of transport organisation. The division of control over transport investment, the possibly different investment criteria that may be adopted in the public and private sectors and the very considerable responsibilities ultimately resting on the government all tend to complicate the investment decision-making process. This is particularly true in Britain's most important form of inland transport, transportation by road. The highly centralised decision-making in road investment, and the very widely dispersed decisions on investment in vehicles, can obviously result in a lack of co-ordination, and a possible misallocation of resources. But this problem is part of a larger issue affecting all forms of investment in transport: this is whether investment decisions should be determined by the market, or should be centrally planned [39]. Although Conservative governments have tended to look to 'competition', and Labour governments to 'co-ordination', to solve Britain's transport investment problems, no government of either party has been prepared to trust wholly either to the market or to central planning. The market solution would involve selling road space, and linking road investment to what people were prepared to pay to use the roads. It would also imply allowing the railways and other publicly owned parts of the transport services to borrow on the market; removing subsidies from the railways; and freeing bus and airline operators from licensing controls. Complete Soviet-style central planning would involve taking virtually all forms of transport into state ownership.

17

The main difficulty in the way of allowing the market mechanism to determine transport investment has been the problem of charging for roads and bridges and other transport infrastructure (an issue which is discussed in Chapters 5 and 6). More recently, the problems of the social costs and benefits of transport services (such as the effect of road traffic on life in towns) that might not be reflected in the workings of the price system have been recognised as being of considerable importance.

Apart from the obvious political difficulties, the main disadvantage of the central planning solution would be the immense complexity of the problems and the near-impossibility of forecasting the demand for the heterogeneous services provided by the transport industry. The ton miles and passenger miles produced by transport undertakings are very far from being homogeneous, and the requirements of different consumers may vary considerably in relation to such factors as speed of journey, comfort, safety or damage level, route followed, distance and regularity.

It is generally assumed by transport economists who have discussed investment criteria that, even where decisions are taken by the government, they should be guided by reference to behaviour in the market. (The only alternative would be to trust in the omniscience of central planners, and there would be very few supporters for such a policy in Britain.) The aims of investment policy could be to maximise either consumers' surplus, producers' surplus or the net total of consumers' and producers' surplus. Maximising consumers' surplus would involve authorising investment that would expand a transport service to the point at which total demand could be met when price was zero. This has the obvious disadvantages that it would probably mean the over-expansion of transport compared with other products and services, and would lead to distortions through the necessity of raising subsidies to cover the losses of undertakings with a nil revenue. There are no serious advocates of consumers' surplus maximisation as an investment criterion. It has been suggested that bus services should be provided free but advocates of zero bus prices do not argue that new investment should be undertaken to meet any resulting excess demand but rather that further contraction of the industry should be

18

prevented. The maximisation of profits, which is achieved by expanding output to the point where marginal revenue equals marginal cost, is in effect the criterion adopted by road haulage undertakings. Competition has generally been too great in the provision of road haulage services for the emergence of the restricted-output, high-price industry that can result from profit maximisation with imperfect competition.

Although the term 'producers' surplus' is used here, because it has figured in discussions of transport investment criteria, it should be noted that the concept can be confusing. Producers' surplus is generally defined as the area below the price line and above the product supply curve, or short-run marginal cost curve, for a firm in a competitive industry. But the term 'producer' can be taken to mean either the owners of a firm or the owners of the factors of production employed, some of which, like labour, are not 'owned' by the firm. There are also ambiguities in the measurement of producers' surplus. Mishan has argued convincingly that producers' surplus is merely a form of economic rent and that the term should be discarded [49]. The total 'surplus' that may be divided between consumers and producers is now generally described as economic surplus.

Gwilliam has followed Hicks in calling the maximisation of the net total of consumers' and producers' surplus, or 'producing to the point where price just ceases to exceed marginal cost', a form of 'social surplus' policy [39]. Foster has recommended a somewhat different investment criterion for transport services supplied by the public sector. This is the maximisation of consumer's surplus 'subject to the requirement that consumers should pay the average private cost of any service they use' [36]. These alternative theoretical aims for investment policy can be examined by developing a simple model of a bus undertaking. Although the figures used in this model are imaginary, they have been chosen to approximate to the cost and demand situations that might be found in the real world [62]. Suppose that the 'Beta Bus Company' was faced with the linear output–revenue relationship

$$AR = 44 - 4 \cdot 25 V$$

where AR is average revenue in pence and V is annual output in million of vehicle miles.

Total revenue (TR) would therefore be given by:

$$TR = 44V - 4 \cdot 25V^2$$

and marginal revenue (MR) by:

$$MR = 44 - 8 \cdot 5V.$$

The cost–output relationship of the bus company is assumed to consist of two linear sections with constant marginal costs of 17p per vehicle mile up to an output of three million vehicle miles, and then to have marginal costs increasing constantly by 5p for every extra million vehicle miles of output. Fixed costs are assumed to amount to £240,000 per annum. The cost–output relationships where ATC_1 and MC_1 are average and marginal costs per million miles for outputs of up to three million vehicle miles per annum and ATC_2 and MC_2 are average and marginal costs per million miles for outputs of over three million vehicle miles a year are given by:

$$ATC_1 = \frac{24}{V} + 17$$
$$MC_1 = 17$$
$$ATC_2 = 2 + 2 \cdot 5V + \frac{46 \cdot 5}{V}$$
$$MC_2 = 2 + 5V.$$

The Beta Bus Company's cost–output and revenue–output relationships are illustrated in Fig. 1. If the company adopted a profit-maximising policy it would produce OV_1 or $3 \cdot 11$ million annual vehicle miles of output. If Beta buses chose to follow the social-surplus-maximising investment criterion they would produce output OV_2 or $4 \cdot 54$ million vehicle miles per annum. If the bus company were publicly owned, and were guided by the constrained consumers' surplus maximising criterion, it would produce OV_3 or $4 \cdot 78$ million vehicle miles a year. Consumers' surplus with social surplus maximisation and marginal cost pricing would be represented by the area ASB and with constrained consumers' surplus maximisation and average cost pricing it would be represented by the area AED.

With this criterion producers' surplus would be zero. Adoption of the social surplus criterion would thus lead to a smaller output (the difference in output levels would be greater if the average revenue curve were flatter and demand more price elastic, or if marginal cost increased more steeply with output)

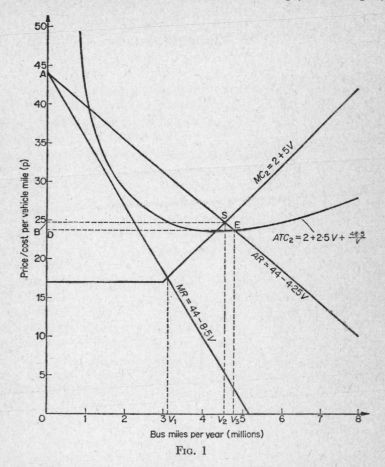

Fig. 1

and would mean that public enterprises would make what might be regarded as an undesirable surplus. The consumers' surplus criterion approved by Foster would fit in with the instruction to nationalised industries to adopt pricing and investment policies based on balancing income and revenue, provided that cost included some allowance for accumulating funds for future investment. But it has the theoretical disadvantage that the marginal cost of the last part of the output (V_2V_3 in the Beta Bus Company example) would be greater than the money people were prepared to pay for it. This situation is analogous to that in the problem of road pricing which is discussed below.

As both Foster and Gwilliam point out there are theoretical and practical difficulties in using either form of consumer surplus criterion as a guide to real world transport investment policy. If investment is made in a public enterprise for the benefit of the community then, it may be argued, it is social rather than private costs and revenue (or benefits) that must be considered. An investment in a new airport in which the cost estimates covered only the direct cost to the airport authority and excluded all consideration of such social costs as the effects of aircraft noise on people living in the area would be unacceptable today. Similarly, a consumer surplus measurement that was related only to the surplus of consumers of the transport industry in which new investment was being considered might be considered inadequate. As was shown in the case of the Victoria Line underground railway investment study, part of the benefit would accrue to road users, if roads became less congested as a result of a transfer of passengers to the new underground line. These people would presumably be prepared to pay for the enjoyment of their increased journey speeds, and this payment should be included in the total of consumers' surplus. A recent survey of the concept of economic surplus concludes that, although there are many objections to its use in policy formulation, it is difficult to find a workable alternative [29].

The consumers' surplus concept is, perhaps, not very well adapted for dealing with social benefits, which may be enjoyed by those who do not appear on the demand curve for the service or good that may have its output increased by new investment. If the Beta Bus undertaking investment were to be determined by the relationship between total cost and benefits, then the two cost curves would have to include social as well as private costs, which in this instance would mean the costs of congestion and wear of the road surface, and the costs of any inconvenience caused to pedestrians and to people living or working on the bus routes. The bus undertaking's private costs

22

would, however, be reduced by the amount of any tax payments involved. Part of these operations would cancel each other out, and the practical problem would be to determine what part of tax payments represented the cost to the state of providing road space for the buses. The social benefits would be

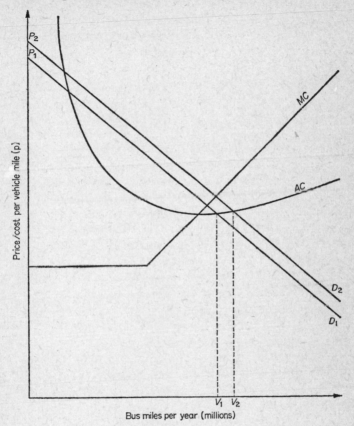

FIG. 2

the value of the time saved by motorists and other road users because the greater use of buses caused a reduction in road congestion. (Although buses add to congestion on the roads a bus with an average peak-hour load of 40 or 50 passengers will make a more efficient use of the road space than an equivalent number of people travelling by car.) Suppose that in the Beta Bus Company case the value of each bus vehicle mile (in

23

reduced congestion cost to other road users) was 2p or P_2P_1 on Fig. 2. The notional new demand curve P_2P_2 could then be drawn and the optimum investment level (according to the average cost = average revenue criterion) would be increased from OV_1 to OV_2 or from an output of 4·78 to 5·19 million vehicle miles a year.

Alternatively, the average cost curve could be replaced by an average social cost curve 2p per unit to the left which would give the same equilibrium positions. The Beta Bus Company costs were based on the assumption that some capital investment (in garages, offices and the nucleus of a bus fleet) had already been made in the past. This would mean that some costs, such as interest payments on capital employed, could not be 'escaped' even if the scale of operations were greatly reduced. If investment in an entirely new undertaking were being considered then all costs would be escapable at the planning stage. This means that (assuming that the units of output under consideration were large enough to make it possible to ignore the added complication of the problem of indivisibilities, and that there were constant returns to scale) average and marginal costs could be regarded as being identical. In these circumstances the social surplus and constrained consumer surplus criteria would both lead to the same amount of investment, but this would still be greater than the optimum investment level for a profit-maximising company with the same revenue–output relationship. If the Beta Bus undertaking were to be started from nothing and had estimated average and marginal costs of £250,000 per million vehicle miles of annual output, then the investment policies approved by Gwilliam and Foster would both imply investment for an output of 4·47 million vehicle miles per annum (considering only private costs and benefits), while the optimum size for a profit-maximising company in the same circumstances would be 2·23 million vehicle miles a year. Once investment had taken place in the bus undertaking, however, some costs would become inescapable in the short run while others would vary directly with output. Marginal and average costs would thus diverge and the social surplus and constrained consumer surplus criteria would lead to different optimum output levels. This anomaly illustrates the importance of relating the concept of escapable and inescapable costs to the time period to which a decision is relevant. This issue is discussed further in relation to pricing in Chapter 5.

Real world transport investment decisions may be considerably complicated by the treatment of past investment. Most capital equipment eventually needs renewal, though the lives of different forms of transport infrastructure may vary considerably. If a sufficiently long view is taken, even rail tunnels may need to be rebuilt, and virtually all transport costs will become variable. There is also a danger that prices will not represent the cost situation accurately if transport undertakings differ in their treatment of past capital expenditure when determining their investment and pricing policies. Some municipal bus undertakings have paid off much of their past capital debt, and the government has allowed the railways to write off a considerable part of their outstanding capital. The fixed costs of British Railways and debt-repaying municipal bus undertakings will therefore appear less than those of transport undertakings, such as road haulage concerns operated by joint stock companies, which may still have all past capital expenditure funded as loan or equity capital, although this financial distinction does not represent any real difference in the use or availability of resources. If the Beta Bus Company had paid off the cost of its original investment in premises and a bus fleet, fixed costs would be reduced or eliminated, and the equilibrium 'average revenue = average cost' point would be moved to a higher level of output.

4 Investment in Practice – Rail, Roads and Ports

Real world transport investment decisions have generally been somewhat uncertainly related to the possible theoretical criteria. There is little information, except what is contained in company reports and statements, about investment in the private sector. There is no reason to believe that the situation is different from that in other industries, however, and it seems likely that the underlying aim of private transport firms is to maximise producers' surplus, though in some cases new investment may be motivated by the desire for growth for its own sake, and sales maximisation may be as important as profit maximisation. Investment policy has been by no means uniform in the public sector, but there has been a development over the past fifteen years from policies that were mainly politically determined, and that lacked any clear economic guidelines, to those that at least demand that there should be a satisfactory rate of return on invested capital. The development of public sector investment policy can be seen most clearly by studying the cases of investment in railways, road track and ports.

A clear critical analysis of postwar investment policy in relation to the railways is contained in Aldcroft's book on British Railways [23]. Between 1937 and 1953 there was very little new rail investment, and maintenance of track, buildings and rolling stock was neglected. It has been calculated by Redfern [58] that there was an effective disinvestment in railways between 1937 and 1953 of £650 millions (at 1960 prices). In 1955 the British Transport Commission published a report *(Modernisation and Re-equipment of British Railways)* which proposed that major new rail investment should be completed. The plan, which it was estimated would cost £1240 million, involved track improvements, the modernisation of signalling systems, the replacement of steam trains by locomotives powered by diesel oil or electricity, the modernisation of stations and the introduction of new, up-to-date passenger and freight rolling stock. The Modernisation Plan was accepted uncritically by the government, and the investment funds were voted to the railways with the minimum of debate in the House of Commons. It was only when it began to be realised that the British Transport Commission's estimate of the expected improvement in the finances of the railways was extremely over-optimistic (a credit balance was forecast for 1962 when the outcome proved to be a loss of £156 million), and when a reappraisal of the scheme showed that the estimated cost must be increased to £1660 million, that serious criticism developed. This increase in cost appears to have been the result of rising prices rather than of faulty estimates [55]. The Select Committee on Nationalised Industries, which reported on British Railways in 1960, was extremely critical of the way in which investment in the Modernisation Plan was approved. The Report stated that

> The Plan was naturally examined by the Ministry of Transport and the Treasury who, as guardians together of public funds, have a joint responsibility . . . The Plan was considered, though not in detail and not on technical grounds; modernisation was desirable, the proposals appeared to be along the right lines, the Plan was flexible and the Ministry gave it their general blessing. There is indeed some difference in tone between the Government's greeting of it at the time as a 'courageous and imaginative Plan' and a Treasury view of it, recollected in tranquillity, as being '. . . merely a hotch-potch of the things that the Commission was saying that it was desirable to achieve by 1970, ill-qualified and not readily explainable' [11].

The members of the Committee were particularly horrified by the revelation that no attempt had been made in the Plan to compare the economic advantage of dieselisation and electrification. Pryke has shown that some rail investment was wasted on services that could not have been made profitable [55].

Since the completion of the Modernisation Plan the railways have generally found it much more difficult to obtain investment capital from the government. There was a complaint in the 1969 Annual Report of the British Railways Board that rail investment was at too low a level and that '. . . too much of the time of the Board's officers is taken up by the need to discuss in detail and justify individual projects with the officers of the Ministry of Transport. The Board feel strongly that . . . the allocation of investment capital within the ceiling should be regarded as their own responsibility' [5]. There was a reference in the 1970 Report to the Corporate Plan for railway development and it was stated that this would require an investment of £517 million, at 1970 prices, over the period 1971–5. Specially mentioned as needing investment (in the 1970 Report) were the London and South East commuter services, the development of the Advanced Passenger Train and the construction of long-wheelbase wagons capable of running at 75 m.p.h. Since the detailed rail arguments for obtaining investment funds are not published it is not possible to say exactly how these are evaluated, but it must be assumed that similar rates of return to those expected from road investment are demanded. It is significant that in the 1969 Report, and more strongly in the 1970 Report, the Railways Board argued that the railways have peculiar social advantages in producing services 'with minimum damage to the environment'.

Until about five years ago there was little attempt to make any consistent economic evaluation of road investment proposals. Even one of the first motorways opened, the M50 or Ross Spur, was constructed mainly because the plans happened to be ready, and it is now clear that many other motorways could have been built which would have shown a higher rate of return than this particular stretch of road. Since Mrs Castle's tenure of office as Minister of Transport, and the appointment of Professor Christopher Foster as the first Director of Economics at the Ministry, considerable efforts have been made to develop appropriate techniques for evaluating road investment projects. This appraisal has, however, mainly been confined to consideration of the allocation of a predetermined amount of investment funds between alternative road projects. The size of these funds is the result of various economic and political considerations and depends upon bargaining between the Department of the Environment, the Treasury and other government departments making claims for investment capital.

The sums allocated to road building are also affected by the general economic situation and by the Chancellor of the Exchequer's views about the need to expand or contract public expenditure.

There are four main classes of roads in Britain – motorways, trunk roads, principal roads and other roads, though the legal distinctions are slightly confused. Motorways were originally given a legal basis by the Special Roads Act of 1949, and their distinctive features are the exclusion of certain types of traffic; the limitation of access and egress points, the absence of frontage development and the existence of defined minimum construction standards. Trunk roads, originally defined under the Trunk Roads Act of 1936, comprise all the main inter-urban through routes in Britain. Principal roads are trunk roads inside urban areas, generally those which run through county boroughs. Some bypass or ring roads inside county boroughs are designated as trunk roads, however, and there are also roads outside county boroughs which are designated as principal roads. In Greater London there are no trunk roads in the former L.C.C. area, but in 1968 there were 152 miles of trunk road in the outer parts of the area now administered by the Greater London Council [17]. The distinction between trunk and principal roads is supposed to be based on whether local or through traffic predominates. The main practical difference is that the central government is directly responsible for the whole cost of building and improving trunk roads and motorways, whereas 25 per cent of the cost of principal road construction or improvement is met by the local authority in whose area it lies (though even some of this 25 per cent may come indirectly from central government funds). All roads that are not trunk roads or principal roads are classified as 'other roads' and are the responsibility of local authorities. The total investment for Great Britain in new construction and improvement of the three classes of road (including motorways with trunk roads or principal roads) in 1969/70 was:

Trunk roads	£206,250,000
Principal roads	£145,762,000
Other roads	£38,910,000

The Department of the Environment is now directly responsible only for roads in England. The Scottish Development Department has been responsible for trunk roads in Scotland since 1956, and the responsibility for trunk roads in Wales was transferred to the Welsh Office in 1965. The allocation of investment funds between England, Scotland and Wales is determined ultimately by the Cabinet, but recommendations are made by the Road Programme Committee, whose main purpose is to review annually the planned expenditure on roads for the next five years. The Scottish Development Department and the Welsh Office are represented on this Committee.

The appraisal of motorway and trunk road investment projects now takes place in two main stages. In the first place, schemes are considered for inclusion in either the Trunk Road Preparation Pool or the Principal Road Preparation List. Preliminary estimates of the costs of projects are made and '. . . whenever feasible, rough cost/benefit calculations are also made to establish the prima facie worth of the potential scheme' (Ministry of Transport memorandum to the Estimates Committee on Motorways and Trunk Roads) [10]. Projects that seem to show an acceptable rate of return are then put into the Preparation Pool, where they are examined more carefully, and feasibility studies may be carried out. Firm cost and benefit calculations are made, and schemes showing the highest rate of return are then transferred to the firm programme of schemes on which work is expected to start in the next four or five years. New roads are added to the rolling programme as work is started on projects that were in the preparation pools. The Department of the Environment aims to have about £1000 million worth of motorway and trunk road projects in the inter-urban preparation pool and a similar amount in the Principal Road Preparation List.

In their main memorandum to the Estimates Committee on Motorways and Trunk Roads the Ministry of Transport claimed that before road schemes are put into the firm programme they are subject 'to full cost benefit analysis' [10], and in the 1970 report on roads in England it is stated that 'Every major inter-urban road scheme is now subjected to cost/benefit analysis' [17]. But the report then suggests that the cost–

benefit techniques are 'under constant review', and it is clear that the techniques are very far from being perfected. The costs and benefits that are measured are the estimated costs of road construction (including the cost of acquiring land and the compensation for any buildings that have to be destroyed) and the costs of maintaining the new or improved road; while the main benefit is the value of the journey time that will be saved as a result of the completion of the scheme. Changes in accident rates and in vehicle operating costs are also estimated, evaluated and added in (usually as benefits) and the total net value of benefits for the first year in which the scheme will operate is calculated as a percentage of the total costs of the scheme. This figure is known as the first year rate of return.

It is obvious that the procedure used by the Ministry and by local authorities at present falls very short of being full cost–benefit analysis. The use of a first-year rate of return criterion means that schemes with a high initial rate of return may be wrongly preferred to schemes where the rate of return is expected to increase over the lifetime of the project. A road improvement in a congested urban area, for example, may give an immediate high rate of return, but this may remain constant or even decline (as congestion builds up again), whereas it may take some years for traffic flows to develop on an inter-urban motorway. The Ministry are well aware of this weakness in current evaluation procedure and have devised a technique for evaluating inter-urban road schemes over a lifetime of thirty years. This scheme involves the use of a computer programme which has been called COBA. The costs and benefits to be measured are the same as those described above, but they are estimated over a thirty-year period. These are then discounted to give the 'present value' of the streams of costs and benefits. Given the discount rate that is agreed for all similar exercises in the public sector, the costs and benefits for the first year after the base date for the comparisons are reduced by the factor $1/(1+r)$. Cost and benefits for the second year are reduced by $1/(1+r)^2$, those for the third year by $1/(1+r)^3$ and so on. The net present value (discounted benefits less discounted costs) is then divided by the capital cost of the scheme, and the schemes with the largest positive ratios are selected. The cut-off point between selection and rejection

31

would depend, of course, upon the size of investment funds available.

The main doubt about the use of the COBA evaluation scheme is whether reasonably accurate forecasts of costs and benefits can be made. It is quite possible that the mistakes that could arise from faulty forecasting might be even more serious than those resulting from using a first-year rate of return criterion. The COBA programme is at present only intended for use with inter-urban road schemes. This is presumably because forecasting traffic flows in urban areas, where a single road improvement may affect flows over a whole network of roads, is even more difficult than with inter-urban roads, and errors in making long-term forecasts may be very considerable indeed.

There has been considerable discussion of the problem of uncertainty in investment appraisal, though it cannot be said that any satisfactory solution that can be easily applied in a real world situation has been found. An analysis of the main contributions to the discussion is contained in Pearce [53]. If probabilities can be given to different levels of benefit being achieved then it is possible, at least in theory, to distinguish the optimum project from a selection of projects with different combinations of expected benefits and attached probabilities. But all major transport investment projects will have unique features, and the probabilities of particular outcomes (e.g. of a specific increase in traffic flows taking place) cannot be determined. The most practical approach is dignified by the name of sensitivity analysis and essentially consists of a recalculation of rates of return on the basis of different assumptions about the values of uncertain variables. This may not be very helpful where the gap between the highest and lowest estimates of rates of return is very great, but in other cases it can clarify decision-making. In the study by Jennings and Sharp [44] on the proposal to apply minimum power to weight legislation to lorries (which would result in gains to the community from reduced delays to other traffic but losses to haulage operators from higher fuel consumption and more expensive engines), there was uncertainty about cost levels. But a sensitivity analysis showed that benefits exceeded costs (for a 6 b.h.p. per ton minimum ratio) both for 'optimistic' and 'pessimistic' estimates of cost increases.

A second major difficulty of the application of cost–benefit techniques to road investment appraisal arises from efforts to put money values on such benefits as time savings and changes in accident rates. A small change in the accepted time evaluation can make a very great difference to the rate of return of any road investment project. These issues of the evaluation of time, human life and other intangibles are of such importance in transport economics that they are discussed separately below in Chapters 8 and 9.

A common and basic problem in the use of cost–benefit analysis is the decision on how many costs and benefits should be included in the calculations. This is certainly met in road investment appraisal, and at least two items of possibly major importance are now omitted from the formal calculations. These are the environmental costs of road schemes, and the long-term developmental benefits that may result from the building of new roads. The importance of the effect on the environment of new roads has become much more widely recognised in recent years, particularly in relation to urban motorways. There are, so far, no accepted techniques for quantifying the environmental costs of roads, and these are dealt with by the 'all or nothing' method of allowing public appeals against the proposed routes for new roads. A major inquiry into problems of motorway and other road construction in relation to the development of Greater London (Greater London Development Plan – Transport) is now taking place and it is to be hoped that this may result in a move towards a more objective and consistent method of measuring environmental costs. Roads in underdeveloped countries are sometimes built ahead of the demand for them, in the hope that the economy of the area served will be greatly stimulated by the new transport facilities and that the traffic flow will build up over a number of years. Although Britain does not have any areas that are completely devoid of transport services, major new roads can nevertheless have a development effect and may encourage new industrial growth. This growth would not be measured in a first-year rate of return evaluation, and even in a thirty-year evaluation the increases in traffic flow will not necessarily measure the development benefits of a road adequately.

The measurement of development benefits involves some

very difficult problems. These benefits will appear only after a considerable period of time, so that studies of the effects of road building, such as that being carried out at Leeds University on the influence of the M62 on industrial growth in Yorkshire and Lancashire, cannot be completed in time to help in the making of current policy decisions. Road building is only one factor affecting regional economic growth and it is not easy to isolate the influence of this particular variable. If increased industrial development in one area is achieved only at the cost of slower growth elsewhere, then this may not represent any real gain to the community. There is also an intangible development benefit of road building in the preservation of existing rural communities, to which it would be extremely difficult to give a money value.

The effects of consideration of development benefits in Britain at present may be (though this cannot be clearly established) to allow more roads to be built in Scotland and Wales than would be the case if rate-of-return measurements were the only criterion. In England new roads now have to be justified by rate-of-return calculations, although these may allow for future growth of traffic flows where long-term measurements are made. There was one major exception to this when it was decided to allocate £50 million to the development of roads in the North-East as a political decision to encourage industry and general development in this area. In Scotland and Wales, however, the rate-of-return criteria have been followed less rigorously and some road investment has been justified mainly on development grounds. The M8 between Edinburgh and Glasgow duplicates an existing three-lane road, the A8, which was not seriously congested, and the estimated rate of return for the motorway was very low. Nevertheless, this road was built because 'its advantage as a link between the two big Scottish cities was recognised as an essential feature of the economic plan for Scotland' (evidence of Scottish Development Department to Motorways and Trunk Roads Estimates Committee).

Another Scottish motorway that has been constructed but would not have been justified by the normal rate of return criteria is the M90 from the Forth Bridge to Perth. Although the long-term development effect of a new road can be regarded

34

legitimately as part of the economic benefits that it will yield, there is a danger that purely political considerations may override the results of economic evaluation in road investment appraisal so long as the development benefits cannot be quantified, but are merely judged subjectively. It also seems that the present division of responsibility for roads in England, Scotland and Wales could mean that the 'development' claims of parts of England (such as the South-West) are less likely to influence the road-building programme than the claims of similar areas in Wales or Scotland. There may be a misallocation of resources if the consumer surplus or the list of benefits to be evaluated is made more extensive for some investment projects than for others.

A final example of the treatment of transport investment problems is that of ports. The methods by which investment funds have been allocated to public sector ports in Britain make an interesting comparison with road investment policy. Recent British port investment policy has been examined in a penetrating critical analysis by Mills [47]. As was the case with road investment, attempts to use economic criteria to evaluate port investment projects are comparatively recent. The Committee of Inquiry into the Major Ports of Great Britain [12], the Rochdale Committee (this must be distinguished from the later Inquiry into Shipping conducted under the Chairmanship of Viscount Rochdale), which reported in 1962, concluded that at that time there was no 'independent economic test of the need for a proposed [port] development scheme'. As a result of the report of this Committee the National Ports Council (N.P.C.) was set up, but this was not given powers to make final investment decisions itself, as the 1962 Report had recommended. Instead, the final decision remained with the Ministry of Transport, but the N.P.C. was able to advise on port investment projects.

As with railway investment, the discussions and studies leading to port investment have generally been unpublished. The main exception was the proposal for a new dock at Portbury in the area of the Port of Bristol Authority. The reasons for the original refusal to sanction this development were published, and for this reason criticism of port investment has centred mainly around the Portbury decision. This does

35

not mean that other port investment decisions might not be equally vulnerable to criticism if sufficient data for a proper critical analysis were available.

The Portbury development scheme was first put forward by the Port of Bristol Authority (P.B.A.) in 1964. The National Ports Council apparently carried out an economic assessment of the project based on figures obtained from the P.B.A. and calculated that the rate of return from the project (which was worked out on a discounted cash flow basis) would vary from zero to 7·7 per cent according to the traffic forecasts, though what they believed to be the most likely traffic forecast gave an estimate at the top of the range. The N.P.C. disclosed in their Annual Report that they had advised the Ministry that investment in the Portbury scheme was justified. One of the reasons for approving Portbury mentioned by the N.P.C. was that it would fit in with the government's plans to encourage industrial development in the South-West. In 1966 the Minister of Transport announced that the Portbury scheme would not be approved, and the reasons were set down in a paper published in October of that year [15]. The main Ministry argument was that the hinterland of Bristol would not provide sufficient traffic to justify the Portbury investment. Figures were produced to indicate that 80 per cent of imports into Britain and 75 per cent of exports from this country do not travel more than seventy-five miles to or from a port. In order to forecast future traffic flows the Ministry used a gravity model which was based on the assumptions that the proportion of an inland region's traffic exported from a particular port will be an inverse function of the distance from the port to the region and a direct function of the total export traffic handled by the port.[1] In both cases

[1] The 'gravity distribution model' has also been used in transport planning to predict traffic flows between different areas or zones; to predict the traffic generated by a new airport; to predict the development of shopping areas; and, indirectly, to measure the value put on travelling time. The assumptions of the model, based on an analogy with the laws of gravity, are that the attractiveness of a zone will vary directly with its size (which will be measured by the appropriate factor, such as the population or number of shops) and inversely with its distance from the zone from which trips originate. A typical model dealing with road traffic flows would seek to measure

36

traffic flows were measured by weight and the same assumptions were made for import traffic.

There are three main points in Mills's criticisms of the Portbury decision. He shows that the basic assumptions of the gravity model are very questionable, and that its powers of predicting traffic flows were limited and liable to wide margins of error. The implication of the gravity model assumptions was that all British ports would receive a constant proportion of any increased traffic flows. This means that no allowance was made for the possibilities that new dock facilities in Bristol would encourage faster economic growth in that area, or that traffic might be attracted away from other ports. The diversion of traffic from other ports does not necessarily involve any gain to the nation, and according to Mills it was a weakness of the N.P.C.'s rate of return calculations that no allowance was made for the possible loss of traffic at other ports. Much of the political objection to the Portbury scheme came from South Wales, as it was Welsh ports that might be most likely to suffer a loss of traffic. (Curiously, the Ministry of Transport's arguments, although rejecting the Portbury investment, did not refer to this possible source of overestimation of benefits in the National Ports Council's figures).

The appraisal of dock investment projects is less difficult than that of road projects in that the investment will result in a cash flow, but Mills argues that this incremental cash flow following new investment may not represent the true gains to the dock users. The charges made by ports take three main forms – dues on ships using the port, dues (levied on a weight basis) on goods loaded or unloaded, and specific charges for the use of port facilities. Mills shows that changes in charges do not necessarily reflect the benefits from improvements in the facilities provided. For example, if the building of a larger dock or dredging operation enabled larger ships to use a port, there might not be

---

the flow of traffic from i originating zones to j destination zones. The total trips made are assumed to be a function of the trips generated by each zone, the attractiveness of the destination zones and the costs of travel between zones, including both money and time costs. There has been considerable criticism of the use of these models.

any corresponding increase in dues paid. The tonnages of goods carried might be constant, though the shipping firms would gain from using bigger ships with lower costs per capacity ton (or per cubic metre). This means that part of the private benefit is left out of the rate-of-return calculations. Mills's third major point is that no attempt was made, with Portbury or with other port investment schemes, to measure the wider range of social costs and benefits that might result. In particular, the relationship of port investment to regional development policy was not worked out.

Some attempts are now being made to improve the techniques of port investment appraisal and to apply cost–benefit analysis to this area of investment. It is obvious that port investment and industrial development are closely related, and the National Ports Council is now interested in the study of Maritime Industrial Development Areas (MIDAs). These are associated port and industrial development areas such as the region around Rotterdam. Professor M. Peston has carried out a preliminary feasibility study for the N.P.C. [21] to find out whether it would be possible to carry out a full-scale cost–benefit study to decide on whether a MIDA should be developed in Britain and where it should be located. He concluded that there was a reasonable case for investing in a British MIDA and that a full cost–benefit analysis was feasible.

Transport investment policy may also be influenced by the source of investment funds. This is a special problem in the public sector and has been discussed mainly in relation to road investment. Morgan [51] has argued that it is an anomaly that road investment, which involves building an asset with a very long life, should be paid for (except for part of the local authority contribution (entirely out of current revenue. Many countries issue some form of road bond to raise funds for road building, and thus draw on resources from the private sector. In discussing the possibility of using loan capital with Lord Chesham (Vice-Chairman of the Royal Automobile Club), the then Minister of Transport argued in 1969 that the methods of finance do not affect the total resources available for road building. While this is certainly true, it does not dispose of the argument that there may be political obstacles involved in raising the level of taxation in order to finance increased road

Investment, whereas borrowing from the public might be less difficult. There is of course the danger that raising loan capital for road building would reduce the supply of capital for other public loan issues. On the other hand, industrialists and others who stood to gain from a speeding-up of the road-building programme might be more interested in bonds that were directly linked to road building than in general Treasury issues. Servicing special road bonds could also create problems, although government tax revenue would increase if the new road-building programme led to increased vehicle mileages. The members of the 1968–9 Estimates Sub-Committee on Motorways and Trunk Roads were sufficiently convinced of the advantages of bringing forward the motorway programme to suggest that the raising of capital by the issue of road bonds, which would be serviced out of general current revenue, should be investigated by the Ministry of Transport. This advice was not accepted by the government, however.

Walters [68] has discussed the desirability of earmarking revenue for a 'road fund' and has concluded that 'there are no marked disadvantages to this form of control', although there is always a danger that funds may be raided, as happened in Britain, and the success of a road fund operation must be related to the nature of the taxes that support it. The National Roads Board in New Zealand constructs and maintains roads from earmarked tax revenue. This has worked well in so far as a regular and substantial expenditure on roads has been guaranteed, but the Board's activities have been restricted by the refusal to grant it borrowing powers. As in so many other countries, the demand for road investment in New Zealand has also been distorted by the restrictive licensing of road goods vehicles.

The main problems of transport investment are, then, the difficulties of forecasting demand, of measuring the value of benefits, of co-ordinating with regional development policy and of making allowance for environmental factors. The nature of the institutions controlling transport investment, the division of transport between the public and private sectors and the methods by which investment capital becomes available are also factors having an important influence on the determination of the pattern of investment in transport services.

5 The Theory of Pricing

Recent discussion relating pricing theories to transport has generally distinguished between the pricing of 'infrastructure' and that of final transport services [57]. The meaning of 'infrastructure' has not always been clearly defined, but it is usually assumed to be capital equipment supplied by the State or some other public authority. Roads, bridges, canals, docks and airports can all be described as transport infrastructure. In discussing infrastructure pricing, and particularly the pricing of roads, economists have attempted to apply distribution theory to the transport situations and to work out an optimum pricing policy. There is of course no reason why this theory should not also be applied to the pricing of capital equipment not supplied by the public sector or to final transport services (such as rail passenger miles or lorry ton miles). The reasons for concentrating on infrastructure pricing seem to have been that this is the special concern of governments, who have sponsored discussion and research, and that there has appeared to be more opportunity for considering the widest social implications where public prices were concerned. The managers of a profit-maximising road haulage undertaking may have to face technical problems (such as the difficulties of measuring the costs of specific operations), but the narrowness of their objective greatly limits the possibilities of varying their pricing policy. There is an additional problem in pricing some forms of publicly-supplied transport infrastructure in that there are practical difficulties involved in collecting payment from users. Some infrastructure (such as street lighting) may have the nature of a 'public good' whose enjoyment by one person does not prevent it from also being enjoyed by others [69]. It may be impossible to charge individuals directly for the consumption of such a service.

As was the case with investment, there is no special body of economic theory applying uniquely to transport pricing. Given the usual assumptions and value judgements it can be shown that the satisfaction of the first and second order conditions for a Paretian optimum position (that the marginal rate of substitution and the marginal rate of transformation for any two goods are equalised) can be reached by setting price equal to marginal cost [69]. Price theory based on Paretian welfare economics was originally concerned mainly with the optimum use of a given capital structure. The extension of this theory to cover changes in the capital structure has involved considerable difficulties in developing satisfactory total conditions. Professor H. Schuster has argued that (price theory has now become schizophrenic in dealing with the maximisation of utility when discussing utilisation of existing resources and with the maximisation of social surplus in relation to investment appraisal) [57]. Social surplus, which is derived from the prices at which consumers will buy and producers will sell, would be the same as total utility only if the marginal utility of money were constant and identical in interpersonal comparisons. This condition is unlikely to be fulfilled in a world of unequal income distribution. (An aspect of this problem is developed below in the discussion of the congestion tax controversy.)

It is possible to make allowance for the distributional effects of investment decisions by applying a system of weights to the benefits (or losses) that will accrue to different individuals or groups. If utility is measured by 'willingness to pay' and the decision-maker wishes to make allowance for the unequal distribution of income, then each £1 of gain or loss for lower-income groups can be weighted more heavily than a £1 change in benefits for higher-income groups. Weights can also be used to alter the relative importance of the gains and losses to different groups according to some social evaluation of what they 'deserve' (apart that is from the income level considerations). Thus, if the costs and benefits of building new road bridges over river estuaries in different parts of the country were being evaluated, 'willingness to pay' data might be weighted to allow for different regional income levels. The government might also decide that some economically depressed areas were particularly deserving and add further weights to allow for this factor. The use of weights involves the problems of deciding how they are to be determined (the use of marginal rates of taxation or of the weights implied by past government decisions are two suggestions that have been made) and of how far they are to be applied in the economic assessment of a project or put in later by the decision-maker. The use of weights based on equity consideration involves making value judgements, but value judgements are also implied if the existing distribution of income is assumed to be optimal or if the income redistribution effects of investment decisions are ignored.

Apart from the philosophical problems of the income distribution issue there are four main difficulties in applying marginal cost pricing to transport infrastructure or services. Firstly, there is the familiar problem of the possible creation of distortions in the economy if marginal cost pricing is used in some areas but not in others. Marginal cost pricing in transport (an industry that is made up largely of undertakings with falling long-run average costs) would tend to divert demand from other sectors of the economy in which prices were based on average cost. Secondly, there is the major difficulty of using marginal cost pricing where there are discontinuities in the production process and output can be expanded only by indivisible 'lumps'. Closely linked with this difficulty is the problem of choosing between short- and long-run marginal cost as a basis for pricing.

These problems are illustrated in Fig. 3. This is based on the imaginary data shown in Table 2 for a transport undertaking (which could be an airline, a bus company, a railway or a road haulier). The output capacity of the undertaking can thus be increased only by indivisible 'lumps' of 20 units, and it has been assumed that long-run costs are falling, while short-run marginal costs (SRMC) are constant. The line marked LRMC

Table 2 Cost data for transport undertaking with cost discontinuities

Output	LRMC (of infra- structure)	LRMC per unit of output range	SRMC (running costs per unit)	Total costs	Average costs
1	1000	50	10	1010	1010·0
20	0	50	10	1200	60·0
21	800	40	10	2010	95·7
40	0	40	10	2200	55·0
41	700	35	10	2910	71·0
60	0	35	10	3100	51·7
61	600	30	10	3710	60·8
80	0	30	10	3900	48·7

represents the long-run marginal cost of additions to the infrastructure *averaged over each output capacity increment of 20 units* with short-run marginal costs added. The average revenue or demand curve is *ar* and total average cost is represented by the series of curves $ac_1 \ldots ac_3$. Social surplus would be increased

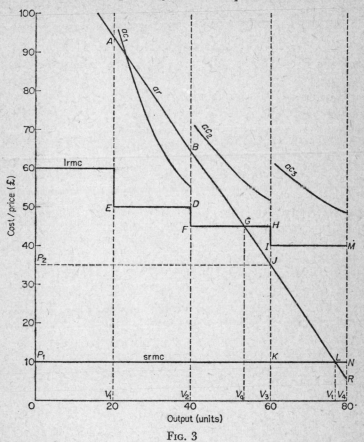

Fig. 3

by expanding productive capacity from $0V_1$ to $0V_2$ (or from 20 to 40 units) since the 'gross' benefit ABV_2V_1 would clearly be greater than the cost increase of EDV_2V_1 and there would be a net gain in social surplus of $ABDE$. The demand and long-run marginal cost curves intersect within the next possible output range at the point G (approximately 53 units of output). But the optimum capacity V_q is unobtainable, the choice being

43

between over-capacity at $0V_3$ (60 units) or undercapacity at $0V_2$ (40 units). With the demand and cost curves shown in Fig. 3 capacity and output should be expanded to $0V_3$ as the gross increase in benefit BJV_3V_2 is greater than the cost increase FHV_3V_2. If the areas not common to both cost and benefit increases are compared it is clear that the social surplus increment BGF is greater than the cost increment GHJ. It would be possible to show a series of demand curves cutting the long-run marginal cost curve between F and H (but nearer to F than to H) for which $0V_2$ would be the optimum output. Capacity should not be increased to $0V_4$ with the relationships shown in Fig. 3, since the extra cost IMV_4V_3 would be greater than the value of the benefits JRV_4V_3.

With the optimum capacity V_3 the price that will just cause all the capacity to be used, and which, in these circumstances, is the optimum price, is JV_3 or $0P_2$ ($=£35$). This is less than long-run marginal cost at this point of HV_3 ($=£45$) but greater than short-run marginal cost KV_3 ($=£10$). The optimum price would be equal to short-run marginal cost if the demand curve sloped more steeply and cut the short-run marginal cost curve before passing the V_3 capacity line.

Suppose that, because of an investment mistake or a fall in demand, the undertaking had invested in equipment giving an output of $0V_4$. The optimum price would then be $0P_1$ ($=£10$) or short-run marginal cost with output $0V_t$ and with the 'surplus capacity' LN unused. The optimum price for a transport undertaking with production discontinuities and falling costs (both features likely to be found in the real world) is therefore likely to be between long- and short-run marginal cost. It will equal long-run marginal cost only if the demand curve happens to intersect the long-run cost curve exactly at a point where the capacity produced by the last unit of investment will all be used. Short-run marginal cost represents a minimum point below which price should never fall. Millward [48], developing a point made by Hirschleifer and Turvey, has argued that the optimum price in the production discontinuity case can be regarded as being equivalent to 'marginal opportunity cost', or the value of resources in their next best alternative use.

The last major difficulty of marginal cost pricing is that its adoption will result in undertakings with falling long-run costs making a loss and needing to be subsidised from some source. There are various 'institutional' barriers to the adoption of marginal cost pricing in declining cost industries. Clearly a falling-cost profit-maximising private enterprise or a public undertaking which has been instructed to break even (raising enough revenue to cover all its costs) cannot base price on marginal cost. Even if loss-making is permissible there are difficulties involved in raising the required subsidy. For publicly owned deficit-making undertakings subsidies must usually be met from general taxation. This increased taxation, whether it is raised as income tax, purchase tax or some more specialised government tax or charge, will itself have economic implications and will disturb the Paretian efficiency conditions. Subsidisation of a particular service from general taxation involves a transfer of income from taxpayers to consumers of the service. The provisions of the 1968 Transport Act for subsidies to support 'unremunerative' rail passenger services means that there is an income transfer from all taxpayers to rail passengers. These transfers are not necessarily harmful, however, since few people would claim that income distribution would be optimal before it was disturbed by subsidy transfers. Obviously, average as well as marginal cost pricing has income-distributive implications. A final problem associated with the subsidisation of loss-making enterprises is that there may not then be any check on managerial efficiency, and losses caused by marginal cost pricing may cover up losses resulting from poor management.

Quite apart from these theoretical objections to marginal cost pricing, there are a number of technical difficulties involved in identifying and measuring marginal costs and in building up an appropriate pricing system. In bus operations, for example, it is possible to distinguish between a number of situations in which marginal costs will differ. On a scheduled bus service the marginal cost of carrying an extra passenger so long as surplus capacity existed would be very low (consisting of fractionally increased fuel costs and a slight lengthening of journey times). If the decision under consideration was whether to make a particular bus trip, then the relevant marginal cost would be the sum of the fuel, repairs, maintenance, tyres, cleaning and maintenance costs involved. The next cost level would add to the costs already listed the cost of the driver's and conductor's wages. This would apply at certain times of the day when there was some alternative work for the driver and conductor, or when the bus crew would have been working on overtime and could therefore be sent home with a consequent reduction in the wage bill. The analysis could be carried further and the situation considered if the 'escapable' marginal cost included a reduction in the bus fleet or in the size of the garage and in the numbers of administrative staff employed [62]. Marginal cost pricing for buses would thus mean having different fares for different routes, and for the same routes at different times of the day or week. It would also involve frequent fare changes as demand conditions varied and as decisions came to be made about the renewal or expansion of capital equipment. The cost of working out and implementing a bus pricing system reflecting all the nuances of marginal cost variation could be considerable and might be as great as the value of the benefits resulting from having a complex and flexible pattern of changes. It has been calculated that a road haulage parcels schedule reflecting the possible combinations of cost factors, even in a very simplified form, would need to contain something like 99,000 separate rates.

6 Pricing in Practice — Charging for Roads

The most important form of transport infrastructure in Britain, as in most countries, is the road system. The theoretical pricing problems that have been discussed can be illustrated by examining some of the main issues involved in charging for road space. Although some countries, notably Italy and the United States, charge directly for the use of motorways, the adoption of a toll system has so far been rejected in Britain. A Ministry of Transport memorandum presented to the Trunk Roads and Motorways Estimates Committee gave reasons for refusing to use tolls [10]. The chief objections were the costs of collection, and the likelihood of diverting traffic to other congested roads with a consequent reduction in the level of the benefits obtained from the tolled road. Work carried out by the Road Research Laboratory suggested that the conversion of an existing motorway like the M1 to toll charging would result in collection costs equal to approximately 25 per cent of the revenue from the toll, though the figure would be lower on a road *designed* to have toll booths. The Ministry memorandum gave official recognition to the existence of consumer surpluses by arguing that tolls paid would not measure the benefit received from a motorway adequately because '. . . the payment of a toll is an indication only of the *minimum* benefit derived by the toll-payer from the facility; in most cases the benefit would be considerably higher' [10]. Tolls are charged on a few major bridges in Britain (Tamar, Severn, Forth) where the diversionary effect is minimal.

Road space is thus provided 'free' in Britain in the sense that there is no direct user charge. The British Treasury has traditionally opposed the 'hypothecation' of taxes, the allocation of taxes to cover a particular form of expenditure, but when a tax falls exclusively on the users of a service supplied 'free' by the State then clearly the yield from this tax should be taken into consideration when the case for making a charge for this service is examined. Road users can thus be said to contribute towards the cost of supplying road space to them when they pay fuel tax and licence duty. Calculations of the yield of these taxes have shown that this considerably exceeds the costs of building and maintaining the roads of Britain. The main source of revenue is fuel tax and it is a peculiarity of this form of 'charging' for roads that it turns fixed costs into running costs. A road haulier must pay tax on fuel consumed and this will vary directly with the mileage operated. His short-tun marginal costs are artificially inflated by the addition of a proportion of fixed costs which do not, in reality, vary with the degree of road usage (except to the extent that road congestion leads eventually to new road building or improvement). The railways, on the other hand, are free to treat track costs more realistically as an overhead expense excluded from their short-run marginal costs.

In his work on charging for roads (which was sponsored by the World Bank and relates, in the first place, to the problems of roads in underdeveloped countries) Walters put forward objections to the use of fuel tax as a means of recovering the costs of providing road space [68]. He argued that it does not distinguish properly between congested and uncongested roads (fuel consumption may be little, if any, higher on a congested than on an uncongested road) and results in over-utilisation of the former and under-utilisation of the latter. Walters argued in favour of marginal cost pricing as the theoretical basis for road charging. Higher charges for the use of congested roads and much lower charges for uncongested roads would not necessarily result in large budget deficits. For uncongested roads he suggested that, given that the zero price suggested by the marginal cost principle may be politically unacceptable, the best tax, in theory, would be one levied on incremental rents. If this proved impossible to administer, he argued that a ton-nage tax would be more efficient than a tax varying with both weight of consignment and mileage, in encouraging economic development in the area served by the road.

Ever since the 1930s there has been a sporadic argument about whether road users in general, and road hauliers in particular, paid a fair contribution towards their 'track costs', or the cost of the road space used by them. In 1964 the British Railways Board published a paper called *A Study of the Relative*

48

True Costs of Rail and Road Freight Transport over Trunk Routes,
which contained the argument that heavy lorries did not pay
their proper share of track costs. This report has been severely
criticised, mainly because the railway's figures were based on
the assumption that the cost of building high-capacity roads
could be reduced by over 70 per cent if they did not have to
carry heavy lorries. This assumption is generally agreed to be
false. A Ministry of Transport study of track costs published in
1968 estimated that, in 1965–6, cars paid charges amounting to
2·1 times the costs of providing and maintaining the roads they
used. Comparable cost–revenue ratios for light vans and heavy
goods vehicles were 1:3·3 and 1:1·8 respectively. For the
heaviest goods vehicles, of over eight tons unladen weight, the
ratio was estimated to be 1:1·6 [18]. A weakness both of this
and similar studies is that the exact relationship between
vehicle weight and road wear has not been clearly determined
as there is a lack of empirical data relating to British road
conditions.

7 The Case for a Congestion Tax

Urban road congestion constitutes one of the most serious transport problems of today. An outstanding general survey of the problems of congestion, consisting mainly of an analysis of the relationship between road widths and design, traffic flows and vehicle speeds, was contained in Professor R. Smeed's inaugural lecture, which has now been published [63]. One method of dealing with the problem of congested urban roads which has been the subject of a considerable amount of recent discussion is the possibility of using the price mechanism to ration scarce road space. The basic case for a 'congestion tax' was set out in a report from a Ministry of Transport Panel, meeting under the Chairmanship of Professor Smeed, which was published in 1964 [16]. The theoretical arguments however were originally developed by Pigou in his discussion of a firm's purchases under conditions of rising costs caused by decreases in the physical productivity of factors of production.

In Fig. 4, C_4D is the demand curve for space on a particular stretch of congested road, while AC and MC measure average and marginal costs. These costs include the time costs of the journey, which increase with traffic flow beyond $0F$ when the road starts to become congested and each additional vehicle slows down all other vehicles. The 'price' paid for the road (vehicle running costs plus time costs) is $0C_2$, with the 'unconstrained' traffic flow $0F_3$. But beyond the point $0F_2$, where the marginal cost and average revenue curves intersect, every additional road user imposes more costs on other road users than the benefits that he obtains from travelling on the road (assuming that these benefits can be measured by what the consumer will pay in order to enjoy them). The costs of extending 'output' from $0F_2$ to $0F_3$ are F_2EGF_3 while the benefits are only F_2EHF_3. Therefore, it is argued, a tax ET should be imposed to reduce traffic flow to $0F_2$.

The Smeed Committee report basically argued in favour of the adoption of a congestion tax, and since 1964 investigations

50

have been made by the Road Research Laboratories into the technical problems involved in collecting such a tax. (It would be necessary to have a meter in cars, which would be activated by electronic impulses.) So far, however, no Transport Minister has been prepared to face the political problems involved in introducing it.

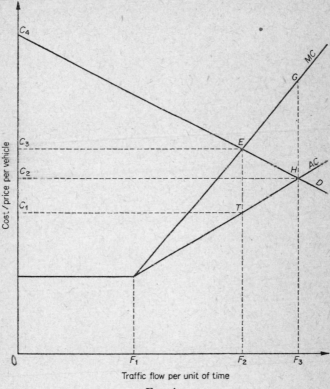

Fig. 4

The desirability of a congestion tax has been widely accepted on the basis of the argument that, if some road users impose greater costs on other road travellers than the benefits that result from their own use of the road, then there would be a clear net gain if the low-benefit users were priced off the road. But some economists have suggested that this argument represents an oversimplification of the situation. [60]. The benefits of road users in the congestion tax argument are measured by the size of the payments (in the two currencies of money and time) that consumers of road space are prepared to make. This measurement of benefit may be a misleading guide to the maximisation of utility or economic welfare unless we are prepared to make the value judgement that income is optimally distributed. The problem is analogous to that met in cost–benefit analysis when the decision must be made as to whether 'willingness to pay' is an adequate measure of the benefits that individuals will secure from an investment project or whether benefits should be weighted to allow for differing marginal utilities of income [53]. Although some degree of inequality in income distribution may be generally accepted in Britain it is also widely agreed that the effects of this inequality on the distribution of some goods and services should be modified by the actions of the State. A case can be made for believing that some adjustments should be made to allow for unequal income distribution when the price mechanism is used to allocate road space. The former users of a road who would be excluded from it by the imposition of a congestion tax would be worse off than before, and would receive no compensation. Their losses may not necessarily be exceeded by the gains of those still using the congested road unless these gains and losses are weighted by different time evaluations, which may simply reflect different levels of income. The income distribution problem is most likely to arise in the case of work journeys, where displaced travellers must find some alternative method of reaching their work place. Fig. 5 represents a situation in which there are two alternative routes, one direct and one circuitous, from a suburban area S to a city centre C, and there is a one-way traffic flow from S to C. Suppose that before the imposition of a congestion tax 10,000 vehicles used the direct route during the morning rush period, taking an average time of 60 minutes for the journey (total travelling time = 600,000 minutes). After the tax was imposed suppose that 5000 vehicles continued to use the direct route and, as congestion was reduced, they completed the journey in an average time of 40 minutes. The other 5000 travellers would be diverted to the longer route and take an average time of 100 minutes for the journey. The overall average travelling time after the tax would then become 70 minutes (total travelling time = 700,000 minutes).

52

Thus if the community accepted the value judgement that, for the journey to work, the time of all travellers should be given equal weight, then the tax would not be imposed. The tax would result in a net gain only if the time of the travellers continuing to use the direct route was valued at a higher rate per minute than the time of the displaced travellers.

This theoretical example illustrates a situation in which the congestion tax solution to road congestion might be rejected. There are many other possible situations in which a congestion tax could have beneficial results without any serious distri-

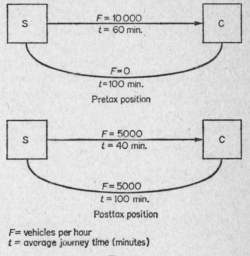

F = vehicles per hour
t = average journey time (minutes)

Fig. 5

butional problems arising. The main possibilities are that some road users without a strong reason to travel in peak periods would not travel at all or would postpone their journey to a different time; that car occupancy rates would be raised; and that the use of public transport would be encouraged and a more efficient use of road space result. (If the journey speeds were increased sufficiently even the displaced car travellers might have quicker journeys than before the tax was imposed). A cogent survey of the possible advantage to be gained from a congestion tax is contained in an article by Professor W. Vickrey [66].

In addition to the basic income distribution problem there

are a number of other difficulties that would be involved in introducing a congestion tax. The Smeed Committee were anxious to avoid asking the government to take the politically unpopular action of increasing the total tax burden on motorists. They suggested that other taxes on motoring (such as fuel tax or annual licence duties) should be reduced, but it has been argued [60] that it would be difficult to do this without partially offsetting the impact of the congestion tax. The cost of collecting the tax would also be considerable and would reduce the size of the net benefits. Some supporters of the case for a tax would like to see it applied also to buses since these add to road congestion though this would tend to conflict with the aid of encouraging the use of public transport [26]. The congestion tax has sometimes been described as an exercise in basing prices on marginal social costs. This is inaccurate, as the tax (in the form proposed in Britain) would not make any allowance for the costs that vehicular traffic impose on pedestrians and on those living and working by the side of roads. The imposition of a congestion tax might even increase some social costs. The nuisance caused by traffic noise, for example, does not become noticeably worse when additional vehicles are added to a heavy traffic flow, and the diversion of some traffic from a congested road to roads that formerly had light flows could increase total noise costs. The general conclusions would seem to be that a cost–benefit analysis of the expected effect of a congestion tax should be made before the tax is applied to any particular set of roads, and that such analyses must be based on clearly defined value judgements about the effect of income distribution on the evaluation of travelling time.

8 The Value of Time

The problem of the evaluation of intangible benefits, which is a common difficulty in applying the techniques of cost–benefit analysis, is of particular importance in transport economics. Any new transport investment in a developed country will normally result in the provision of quicker, rather than of entirely new, transport facilities. The major 'output' of most transport investments will thus be a saving in time (for men, vehicles or goods). In some cases, such as with the introduction of a fast new electric rail service, it may be possible to find out how much money people will pay in order to reduce their journey times. But for investment in roads and other forms of transport infrastructure where the 'product' is not sold directly to consumers, it is necessary to put some value on time savings if any estimates of rates of return are to be made. A recent calculation of the costs and benefits expected to result from a proposed urban road construction and improvement scheme (the Granby Halls project in Leicester) was based on estimates of three main factors: net reductions in journey times, reductions in accident rates and increases in road maintenance costs. The estimated figures were:

	Benefits or costs: £ per peak hours	% of gross benefits
Net time changes	+ 263·409	96·4
Reduction in accidents	+ 9·716	3·6
Increase in road maintenance costs	− 3·773	
Net benefit	269·352	

Time savings alone may be expected to make up about 90 per cent of the value of the benefits resulting from a typical transport investment. The theory and practice of the evaluation of time savings has thus become a major concern of transport economists.

The practice currently recommended by the Department of

the Environment[1] is to divide time savings into two main categories, savings in working or business time, and savings in leisure or non-working time [49]. Working time covers all journeys made when travellers are earning their living. Commercial travellers, businessmen or service engineers travelling during the working day, and bus drivers and lorry drivers at their work are all considered to be using up working time. All other journeys, including commuting to and from work, are assumed to be made in leisure time. The basis adopted for valuing working time is average earnings, plus insurance payments and any other costs incurred by employers that are directly related to the employment of a particular worker. This approach is based on the marginal productivity theory of wage determination and the assumption that earnings (plus other employment costs) per unit of time represent the value of the marginal product of each worker [41]. This means that if a worker who costs his employer £1 an hour can save working travelling time of half-an-hour, this time saving will be worth 50p to the employer (either because the worker will be employed for a shorter total period or because he will produce additional output valued at 50p in the extra thirty minutes available).

Leisure-time values have not usually been related to any particular basis of economic theory but have been derived

[1] In road investment evaluations at the time of writing, many local authorities were still using standard time values for an 'average' composition of traffic and mixture of leisure and business travellers, which might or might not be appropriate to the actual conditions on their roads. These values were derived from the formula:

$$C_m = 1 \cdot 79 + \frac{95 \cdot 8}{v} \quad (v < 38 \text{ m.p.h.})$$

where C_m is the 'cost of delay' (time costs plus running costs) per vehicle mile in new pence. This formula, which is explained in a pamphlet published in 1968 (*The Economic Assessment of Road Improvement Schemes*, R. Dawson, Road Research Laboratory, Technical Paper No. 75) and which is the basis of figures in more recent Department of the Environment circulars, assumes that leisure time should be valued at 75 per cent of working time, not at 25 per cent as is now thought to be appropriate.

from various studies of people's behaviour in situations where they could choose between slower and cheaper and faster but dearer forms of transport. This is generally described as the behavioural or revealed preference approach to leisure time evaluation. Some time values have been obtained as a byproduct of models constructed to analyse 'modal choice' or the factors affecting the ways in which travellers chose between different modes of transport such as bus, car, rail or air. Studies of the value of leisure time made in Britain include those by Beesley, Quarmby, Lee and Dalvi, the Local Government Operational Research Unit (LGORU) and Dawson and Everall. Beesley studied the choice between public transport modes and between public transport and private car for the journey to work of Ministry of Transport employees [27]. Quarmby's study was of the choice between car and public transport for car owners travelling to work in central Leeds [56]. A sophisticated discriminant analysis model was used to estimate the influence of a number of factors (such as travel time, cost, percentage of walking time) on modal choice.[1] Discriminant analysis was also used in the LGORU study, which dealt with modal split for work journeys in Liverpool, Manchester, Leicester and Leeds [46]. Lee and Dalvi's study dealt with the choice between different public transport modes [46]. Travellers were asked what increase in price on the modes of transport they used would make them indifferent between this mode and the alternatives. The respondents in the sample were found to divide into 'time preferrers', who would choose the quicker but more expensive modes of transport, and 'money preferrers', who tended to do the opposite. Dawson and Everall's study, published in 1972, was based on the choice made by motorists between free but relatively slow ordinary roads and tolled autostrade [33]. Two routes were selected in which, in each case an autostrada and an ordinary multi-purpose road were the only alternatives available to motorists. One route, of 147 km, was from Rome to Caionello on the Autostrada del Sole and the other, of 162 km, from near Milan

[1] Discriminant analysis is a technique for allocating observations, which might have come from either of two populations, with a minimum of error. See M. G. Kendall, *A Course in Multivariate Analysis*, Griffin, 1957.

to Modena. A form of regression analysis such as logit analysis is used.[1] The explanatory variables were the differences in journey times and costs (assumed to be equal to the autostrade tolls) on the two pairs of routes.

From this and similar research work certain general points about the value of leisure time can be deduced. Most studies showed that there is a relationship between the valuation put on time savings and income. Thus Beesley found time savings to be valued at 30–50 per cent of hourly income, Quarmby at 20–25 per cent and Lee and Dalvi at 15–45 per cent. The average value in the LGORU survey was 24 per cent for time spent in vehicles but there was very great variation between different towns according to this study, 'in vehicle' time being valued at only 14 per cent of the hourly wage rate in Leeds but at 98 per cent of the wage rate in Leicester. The Dawson and Everall autostrade study found values for commuting and other non-work journeys of approximately 75 per cent of the average wage rate. A clear finding of these studies is that savings in different types of travelling time are valued differently. People apparently dislike waiting for a bus or train, or walking, more than they dislike travelling time spent in a car or bus. The LGORU study, for example, showed that (using pooled data for the four towns) 'in vehicle' time savings were valued at 16p an hour, waiting time at 27p an hour and walking time at 38p per hour. (In Leeds and Manchester savings in waiting time were valued more highly than savings in walking time.) Some studies, such as Beesley's pioneering work, have not differentiated between the alternative ways in which travelling time can be spent, and this may account for the time value differences found (studies having a relatively high proportion of waiting or walking travelling time would be expected to give

[1] This measures the probability that the dependent variable will possess a particular attribute, which in this study was that motorists would travel by autostrada. The analysis assumes the the probability is given by

$$\frac{1}{1+e^{-L}}$$

where L is a linear function of the independent variables.

higher values than those relating wholly or mainly to 'in vehicle' time).

Many of the studies of time-saving evaluation have related only to commuting time. Evidence on the value of time savings of those who are neither working nor travelling to or from work is, at present, very inadequate. On *a priori* grounds it is apparent that there will be very considerable variations in the value of this form of leisure time. A man travelling to meet his girlfriend may value a time saving very highly, whereas time savings for Sunday afternoon motorists may have a negative value; people may prefer motoring to any alternative use which they could make of their Sunday leisure time.

On the basis of the empirical evidence available the Department of the Environment (D.O.E.) use a figure for non-working time of 25 per cent of average hourly wage rates, which is approximately equal to 19 per cent of household income (expressed as an hourly rate for a forty-hour week). Working time values by the D.O.E. [40], [41] are (1969 price level):

	p
All workers	110·4
Car drivers	122·5
Rail passengers	131·7
Bus passengers	63·75
Heavy goods vehicle drivers	52·5

The differences represent different income levels. Average 'all workers' figures are normally used for the whole country. If regional working-time values were calculated on this earnings basis, some regions, such as the South-East, would have higher values than others. The use of national average values implies accepting the value judgement that the 'rich man's pound' and the 'poor man's pound' should be given equal importance in transport investment appraisal, and that it would therefore be wrong to build relatively more roads in the more prosperous regions. In practice, as has been shown in the discussion of investment earlier in this book, the opposite policy is followed to some extent, and extra investment allocated to 'development' areas which would have low average time values.

The Roskill Commission report on the siting of the third

London airport used time values based on a study of the earnings of passengers travelling to Heathrow and Gatwick airports [22]. This resulted in business earnings being valued at 231·25p since businessmen travelling by air have high average incomes. Non-working time was valued at 22·5p or 25 per cent of the income of 'leisure' travellers in the sample.

The Roskill research team adopted Department of Environment practice in using the figure of 25 per cent of income. The difference in travelling time costs to the different airport sites was a crucial factor in preferring the inland sites to Foulness, and the Roskill time evaluations have been widely attacked. Partly to meet this attack, high and low time values, 50 per cent above and below the figures resulting from the Gatwick and Heathrow survey, were used in the final Roskill cost–benefit calculations. The debate on time values in the Roskill inquiry illustrates the lack of agreement that exists. In one case the same research results were used to support contradictory arguments, and widely differing time values were suggested. Professor N. Lichfield, for example, argued that leisure time should be valued at only 2·5p an hour, while some of those submitting evidence appeared to believe that leisure time savings had no value at all for air passengers [22].

Although the evaluation of working time is more firmly based on economic theory than is that of non-working time, there are nevertheless some problems here also. The most important objections to the practice of using wage rates to measure the value of working time are that the labour market is imperfect, and earnings do not measure accurately the value of labour in alternative uses; that time savings caused by transport improvements cannot in practice be used to increase output; that travel time may itself be used productively (businessmen may read documents or draft letters); and that valuing travel time only from the viewpoint of the firm or employer ignores its utility or disutility to the traveller himself [41]. A curious result of using labour costs as the sole determinant of working-time values is that in the D.O.E. figures the value of time derived for light goods vehicles is slightly higher (127 old pence) than that for heavy goods vehicles (126 old pence). This is because light vehicles have a higher occupancy rate, but it is surprising that delaying a consignment of, say, twenty tons is counted as less costly than delaying one of only two tons.

The problem of using working-time savings is considered below in the discussion of the relative value of small and large savings. The objection about ignoring the utility of savings of working-time travel to the travellers themselves is important because it raises a basic theoretical issue. The wages approach assumes that working-time savings are valued only for the extra contribution that can be made to G.N.P. The 'total utility' approach, which is the same as that used in cost–benefit analysis, involves considering the relative utilities that *employees* attach to travelling time and working time as well as its value to employers. This approach is undoubtedly more satisfactory theoretically but has the disadvantage that there is no simple way of measuring the utility or disutility of travelling time to employees. So far little work has been completed on attempting to measure the value put on working-time travel directly in the way that revealed preference studies have sought to evaluate leisure-time travel savings.

Some attempts have been made to develop a theory of the value of time (not only travelling time) based on neoclassical consumer theory in which conditions are found for maximising utility when a consumer has to choose between alternative forms of consumption and is subject to a budget constraint. G. Becker has constructed a theory of the allocation of time developed partly from his work on the use of time in education and other forms of training [25]. He argues that the full costs of goods should include both market prices and the cost of time used in their consumption. He regards households as 'producing units' that combine time and market goods to produce 'basic commodities', which they then choose in such a way as to maximise utility. Times can be converted into goods by working longer hours and forgoing time spent in consumption: the total resource constraint, in Becker's utility-maximising model, becomes the maximum money income that could be earned if the minimum possible time were devoted to any activity except work. This 'full income' can be spent either on market goods or, indirectly, by forgoing money income for leisure or consumption activities. More recently DeSerpa has developed a 'theory of the economics of time' which builds on Becker's model but adds the important point that people can choose to

61

spend a longer or shorter time in consumption (above a fixed minimum period) [34]. Where people are free to use up more than a minimum time at a consumption activity, then the time constraint is no longer effective. Alan Evans has shown that in some theoretical work on the value of time there has been confusion between the value of changes in the total time available and the value of being able to spend time in any particular activity [35]. It is debatable whether the total supply of time can be changed in any meaningful way; in certain circumstances men may be able to pay to extend their lives, but no one can add a twenty-fifth hour to the day. The value of transport-time savings depends upon the relative values put upon different uses of a fixed supply of time. Suppose that a utility-maximising model in which an individual can allocate his time between costless activities (like going for a walk), activities for which he is paid and those for which he must pay is subject only to a total time constraint and to a budget constraint. Then the utility-maximising position can be represented by the equation

$$u_i - \lambda r_i = \mu \qquad (i = 1 \ldots n)$$

where u is the individual's marginal utility obtained from spending time in the ith activity, λ represents the marginal utility obtainable from relaxing the budget constraint, μ is the marginal utility derivable from relaxing the time constraint and r_i represents the payment made or received for the ith activity. (r_i is positive if the consumer pays for the activity, negative if he is paid for it and equal to zero if the activity is free.) In this case a marginal saving of travel time would be of no value to a consumer who had allocated his time optimally. If the consumer transfers a small amount of time from travelling to working then he is exactly compensated by the payment made to him (which means that r_i is negative in this model); if he uses the time saving for a leisure activity for which he must pay (like visiting a theatre) then the utility from this activity is exactly balanced by the payment that he makes. In neither case is the consumer better or worse off (nor would he gain if the time were used for a 'costless' leisure activity). This result, as Evans points out, conflicts with the empirical evidence that people behave as if a travel-time saving made them better off. The contradiction arises because the assumption of the model that people are free to allocate time in very small amounts to any activity is no true. Certain activities (as DeSerpa [34] and Becker [25] have also shown) require a minimum consumption of time. Evans has developed a utility-maximising model for consumer's behaviour in relation to the evaluation of travelling time in which a third constraint, the essential travelling time associated with a particular activity, is added. This amended model can be reduced to the expression

$$\frac{K}{\lambda} = r_t - \frac{u_t - \mu}{u_w - \mu} \, r_w$$

where K is the marginal utility obtainable from a relaxation of the constraint on the allocation of time to travelling (i.e. from a travel-time saving), λ as before is the marginal utility from relaxing the budget constraint, r_t is the money cost of travelling, r_w is the wage rate (which is negative as in the two-constraint model), u_t and u_w are the marginal utilities of travel and work time and μ is the marginal utility of leisure time.[1] It follows from the arguments developed by Evans and others that the marginal utility of leisure time is not equal to the marginal utility obtained from earnings except in the special case where the marginal utility of time spent at work is zero.

An important issue which has not been satisfactorily determined is whether small time savings should be given the same value per unit as larger time savings. If a time saving of one hour is valued at £1·20, does it necessarily follow that a time saving of one minute is worth 2p or that a saving of thirty seconds would be valued at 1p? Evans has argued that 'time savings are only of value if the individual can transfer the time saved to some other activity which he prefers' [35]. The ability to use a time saving for a preferred activity may be influenced by the size of the saving. A commuter might prefer playing tennis to travelling home from work but be indifferent between travelling and waiting at home for his evening meal. A time saving large enough to enable him to play a set of tennis before

---

[1] K, λ and μ are Lagrange multipliers used in finding the maximum value of functions that are subject to constraints.

eating would thus have higher unit value than a small saving which merely extended his 'meal waiting time'. Similarly, thirty minutes more time at work might be capable of being used productively, when an extra five minutes in the office might not. Tipping [64] and others have contended that small time savings may have zero value. The main argument against giving zero value to small time savings depends upon the contention that if time can be used only in indivisible lumps, then some travellers must have unusable 'surpluses' of time. Each small time saving will convert some of these surpluses into usable lumps of time and the total increment of usable time may be equivalent to the total 'crude' time savings. If it is assumed that travellers on a particular route are evenly distributed amongst the possible ranges of time surpluses it can be shown that 'crude' and 'usable' time savings are identical. Suppose that there are 1000 business travellers using a road on which there have been a series of journey time improvements of five minutes, and that, for all the travellers, the minimum usable 'lump' of time is twenty minutes. Then, on the even distribution assumption, there would be fifty travellers with zero 'surplus time', fifty with one minute surplus and so on. A new five-minute time saving would convert the unusable surpluses of 5×20 travellers into usable time 'lumps' of twenty minutes per travellers, so that the total increment of usable time would be $5 \times 50 \times 20 = 5000$ minutes. This is the same as the total 'crude' time savings of 5×1000 minutes. Whether this argument applies to very small time savings of less than about five minutes may be doubted, as the behaviour of travellers might be satisfactorily adjusted to use very large surpluses of time. (In other words the assumption that time can be used only in lumps of an exactly determined size may be unrealistic). Even in cases where it is believed that time savings are too small to be used for any economic activities, it does not follow that these should be given zero value. They may still have some value if the disutility of some unpleasant form of travel is reduced.

The Roskill research team, while arguing that small time savings should be given a full unit value, nevertheless recalculated the cost–benefit comparisons with small time savings given a zero value. Their estimates showed that if time savings of less than five minutes were given zero value the benefits of inland sites compared with Foulness would be reduced by less than 12 per cent, while if savings of less than ten minutes were considered worthless the reduction would amount to 2·5 per cent [22]. For urban road investment, however, the effect of devaluing small time savings could be much more important. In the case of the Leicester Granby Halls scheme (which has already been mentioned), reducing the unit value of time savings of three minutes or less to 25 per cent of that of a fully valued period would cut the estimated first-year rate of return from 19·7 per cent to 5·3 per cent. If the present practice of giving the same unit value to all time savings is wrong, this means that the rate of return from urban road investment (when small time savings may be enjoyed by a large number of travellers) could be overestimated compared with the return from inter-urban road investment where traffic flows may be lower but individual time savings greater.

9 The Value of Life and of Accident Prevention

Transport investment and transport policy decisions will both have an effect on the level of the accident rates of travellers. For most forms of investment in transport infrastructure, the benefits from reductions in accident rates will be relatively small compared with the value of time savings, though it is nevertheless important that they should be measured with some degree of accuracy. For policy decisions on such issues as the imposition of road speed limits or the framing of regulations for air traffic control, and for specalised investment in such items as street lighting or marine radar equipment, the expected benefits from accident reduction are obviously all-important. The valuation of accident reduction has thus become a major concern for transport economists.

Most of the work carried out on the cost of travel accidents in Britain has related to road accidents, and these are made the main subject of the discussion, though the issues involved apply equally to accidents on other transport modes. Road accidents can be divided into three main types for costing purposes: there are those causing damage to vehicles or property, personal injury accidents and fatal accidents. The valuation of 'damage' accidents is mainly a problem of the collection of data since the cost of repairs or replacement and loss of output are monetary costs which can be measured directly. Insurance claims provide an important source of information on the cost of damage accidents. Some allowance must also be made for possible costs incurred by the police and for legal costs.

The greater part of the cost of injury accidents can also be estimated by measuring the costs of medical treatment, of loss of output and of the services of the police, lawyers and insurance administrators. But there is clearly also a subjective cost associated with injury accidents. Most people would presumably pay something to avoid the unpleasant experience of being involved in an accident (and this would apply even to a damage-only accident) and to escape any pain or inconvenience resulting from an injury. The costing of road accidents in Britain is now based on two reports by R. F. Dawson ([30], [31]) of the Transport and Road Research Laboratory (which were developed from earlier work by D. Reynolds). The earlier, 1967, report included an arbitrary sum of £200 for the 'subjective' cost of a serious injury accident and this was increased to £500 in the 1971 report, while that for a slight injury accident was raised from zero to £10. There is still no allowance made for the disutility of being involved in a non-injury accident.

The greatest difficulties in evaluating the cost of accidents is in dealing with those resulting in death. The problem of giving a money value to human life is, of course, important in many other issues besides that of the evaluation of fatal transport accidents. Work on the value of life has been related, in particular, to the evaluation of public health programmes.[1] One approach to the problem is to say that the cost of a death is not less than the loss of the output which the deceased person would have produced. In Dawson's report the average discounted value of output during the expected lives of people killed in road accidents was calculated. The average was weighted according to the ages of people killed in a sample of fatal road accidents. It is sometimes argued that if society loses an accident victim's output, it also gains the consumption that he will no longer need. In the earlier Dawson report a net output figure was calculated, the value of saved consumption being deducted from that of net output. This gave the figures for the narrowly material value of human life for 1965 road accidents as:

$$\text{Males} \quad = \quad +\pounds 4360$$
$$\text{Females} \quad = \quad -\pounds 1120$$

Since the work done by housewives was given a low value in the calculations, society could be said to gain on average (from what Dawson called 'a strictly material point of view') when women are killed in road accidents.

It is obvious that human life also has a subjective value in

[1] See, for example, B. A. Weisbrod, *Economics of Public Health: Measuring the Economic Impact of Diseases,* University of Pennsylvania Press, 1961.

addition to that of net output. Most people want to go on living and would pay to be saved from premature death. Potential accident victims also have friends and families who would suffer from much more than an economic loss if the accident were allowed to happen. Society is demonstrably prepared to use resources to prolong the lives of those who no longer make any contribution to G.N.P. Dawson tacked the problem of the subjective value of life by assessing it at an arbitrary figure of £5000. The only justification for this figure was that it was sufficient to give a positive value to life savings in all age groups even when non-paid work such as housewives' services was not valued. (If only paid work is valued the average net loss from a female fatality in the 0–4 age group was estimated as being −£4560).

The net output approach to life evaluation has been criticised by those who argue that consumption should not be deducted from expected earnings. If a person whose life may be saved by accident prevention methods is considered to be a part of society, and if benefits are measured after the fatal accident has been prevented, then he is alive to enjoy his consumption and, it is argued, consumption should not be deducted from the value of output. It is certainly true that the difference between output and consumption (i.e. the net addition to capital stock resulting from a person's life) is a very inadequate method of valuing human life. But, as Beesley and Evans point out, in what is currently the most recent and comprehensive study of the costs and benefits of road safety measures, it is not at all clear that measurement of the value of gross output gives us the right figure, either [28]. No one would surrender the whole of his future income to escape a fatal road accident, unless he happened to have a preference for death by starvation. A possible solution would be to deduct from income only the cost of a minimum level of subsistence instead of that of average expenditure on all consumer goods and services. Income net of the expenditure necessary to maintain life at a standard just above that at which we might feel that we are 'better off dead' would, perhaps, be what most people would pay, from their own resources, to escape accidental death.

But this private value of a saved life might differ from that which society judged to be appropriate. Most people would probably accept the judgement that the lives of poor and rich men should be given equal value, so that individual evaluations must be adjusted upwards or downwards to an average level. Secondly, and more importantly, society may, in effect, be prepared to augment the sum an individual would pay to save his own life, the addition representing the emotional loss which some of those still alive would suffer from his death. If a man had to pay a ransom to save his life, he would normally to able to add gifts from his family and friends to his own resources (whose maximum value would be his savings plus loans made against his expected future earnings). The reduction of the death rate through accident prevention is essentially an exercise in marginal life saving. Society can thus afford, if it wishes, to use resources for investment in accident prevention measures that are greater than those which those whose lives are saved could themselves command. The argument can be illustrated from the ransom example. If the probability of being compelled to pay a ransom to save your life was very high then the likelihood of obtaining gifts from others to make up the ransom money would be reduced. Even if the average sum that a man could produce from his own resources to pay to save his life were only £10,000, the state might be prepared to spend more than £75,000,000 a year to save the lives of the 7500 people (1969 total road deaths = 7365) killed in road accidents. The likelihood that society would pay more than £100,000 to save the lives of 10 people is even greater. On the other hand, it would be quite impossible for the state to pay as much as £540,000,000,000 to provide protection for all those who might be killed in a nuclear war. In countries where the overpopulation problem is taken seriously the reverse situation might exist, and then the social benefits from saving a life could be valued at a lower figure than private benefits.

In Dawson's second report, on which official accident evaluations policy is currently based, the cost of fatal accidents was increased from £9270 (1965 prices) to £16,980 (1968 prices) by discontinuing the practice of deducting the value of consumption. (Averaged over all accidents this change causes cost increase of 10 per cent [31].) Life is thus valued as the total discounted value of expected output plus the arbitrary sum of £5000. The 'gross value of output' approach is based on the assumption that the proper value of life is what a man would himself pay to avoid a fatal accident, and it appears to be illogical to continue to add in the £5000 'subjective' value for a life when consumption is not deducted from output. Dawson himself suggests that his revised figures may involve some double counting.

Another approach to the life evaluation problem has been based on the argument that what ought to be measured is the value put on a reduction in the probability of suffering a fatal accident. Schelling [59] has supported this view and argued that a man's earnings are not necessarily directly related to what he would pay to reduce the possibility of suffering a fatal accident. Attempts to evaluate these changes in accident probabilities have led to studies of behaviour in choice situations similar to those adopted in the revealed preference approach to time-saving evaluation. Professor L. Needleman, for example, is examining the 'danger money' payments that are made to some building workers (on high scaffolding) and relating these to the degree of risk involved in this work. Jones-Lee [45] has attempted to use von Neumann–Morgenstern techniques to measure the preference of individuals in a trade-off between income, leisure and different levels of risk of death in a road accident. The technique involves finding the odds at which an individual would be indifferent between a gamble (with the alternative outcomes of death in a road accident or enjoying a very high level of both income and leisure) and the certainty of a relatively low income–leisure level but a zero probability of death in a road accident. This approach avoids the difficulties associated with the interpretation of empirical evidence, but is open to the objection that people may not behave in reality in the way that they say they will when answering the hypothetical questions of a von Neumann–Morgenstern experiment. All attempts to base the cost of fatal accidents on estimates of the value of small changes in the probability of their occurrence meet the difficulty that the relationship between the value of small and large changes in the probability of being killed may not be linear. Some people may be prepared to pay large sums to avoid high risks and yet actually enjoy a *slight* risk of suffering a fatal accident. Finally, all revealed preference approaches imply either that there is no difference between the social and private valuations of a saved life, or that the private value is more appropriate.

10 The Impact of Government

It is impossible to examine the economics of transport operation in Britain without discovering the results of government activity. As has already been shown, the government provides directly or indirectly a large part of the infrastructure for road, rail and air services, and it also provides final transport services through the operations of British Rail, the National Freight Corporation, the Docks and Harbours Board, the National Bus Company and the airway corporations. The government's fiscal policy has an important effect on road and rail transport. Fuel tax increases the cost of petrol and diesel fuel by 500–600 per cent. The total estimated cost of operating a thirty-two-ton lorry in 1968 was 16·54p per mile: 3·69p, or 22·3 *per cent* of this cost, was represented by fuel tax. Cars and lorries also have to pay licence duties, and new cars are subject to purchase tax. Part of this tax burden may be regarded as a charge for the provision of the roads, but there is undoubtedly a pure tax element (see the previous discussion on track costs). The railways are treated quite differently. Their fuel is exempt from taxation, and passenger services receive a direct government subsidy under the 1968 Transport Act. This subsidy (together with the grant for 'surplus track') amounted to £73·6 million in 1970 [5]. It is obvious therefore that government taxation policy must affect the relative level of demand for road and rail services.

Since the 1930s (1930 for buses and 1933 for lorries) the government has regulated the operation of bus and road haulage services by controlling entry to these industries through a licensing system. But licensing was originally designed to eliminate 'undesirable' competition between bus undertakings and to protect unremunerative services on less densely populated routes. In return for a monopoly of the bus routes in a particular area undertakings were expected to run some unremunerative services, subsidising these from the profits on the high density routes. This licensing system, although it still exists, is now beginning to break down. The steady decline in the number of bus passengers over the last twenty years has resulted in many

71

undertakings finding that they have insufficient surplus from their profitable routes to meet losses on the unremumerative ones. The institutional pattern has been transformed by the absorption of practically all private bus companies into the publicly owned National Bus Company. In four conurbations (South-East Lancashire and North-East Cheshire; Liverpool; Tyneside and the West Midlands) passenger transport authorities (P.T.A.s) have been set up to operate bus services (through the Passenger Transport Executives) and to co-ordinate road and rail passenger transport. But these new authorities do not have full control of the bus services in their areas (since National Bus Company buses have remained separate), and can do nothing for the rural areas outside their boundaries from which many commuters may travel into the conurbations. Their relationship with British Railways is still not properly developed. The P.T.A.s have been reluctant to use their powers to subsidise rail services and have not had the necessary information to develop a full transport plan for their areas. The P.T.A.s are, however, new creations, and it is too soon to judge what their ultimate impact on conurbation transport will be. In London the Greater London Council has taken over the functions of the former London Transport Executive, and has unique powers to plan passenger transport, and to co-ordinate this with urban development. Outside London and the P.T.A. areas the old licensing system still continues usually, with municipal undertakings operating in the large towns and the National Bus Company being left with services in the outer suburbs, the countryside and in smaller towns. It has been argued that the rigid boundary system, which prevents buses of one undertaking picking up passengers in the area of another, is wasteful and uneconomic. Research in Leicester and Nottingham has shown that rigid boundaries to operating areas result in much poorer bus load factors than could be obtained by an integrated service ([62], [65]).

The licensing of road haulage vehicles was also designed to eliminate 'wasteful' competition. A licence had to be obtained for each vehicle which was to be operated for 'hire or reward' and other road hauliers, or the railways, could object to the granting of any new licence. The applicants had to establish that there was a need for the additional carrying capacity that could not be met by existing services. Traders carrying their own goods could obtain a licence more or less automatically, but they were restricted to carrying their own products or those of a 90 per cent owned subsidiary company. The whole licensing system for lorries was abolished by the 1968 Transport Act, and there is now only one class of licence, the Operators Licence, for all commercial vehicles. Obtaining an Operator's Licence depends only on having maintained vehicles properly and on convincing the Licensing Authority that the applicant possesses adequate financial and managerial resources. Britain is now almost unique amongst developed countries in allowing free entry into the road haulage industry, and in making no distinction between carriage for 'hire and reward' and 'on own account'. It is, however, likely that this freedom will soon disappear, as E.E.C. regulations still insist on preventing own-account operators from competing with road hauliers. The 1968 Act contained provisions for 'quantity licensing' which would have made it necessary to obtain a licence for any long-distance haulage operations. This part of the Act, which was intended to encourage the use of rail, has never been enforced. An important critical review of government policy towards transport as it was worked out in the 1968 Transport Act is contained in an article by Munby [52]. This discusses the licensing changes, urban transport policy, railway policy, road track costs, and passenger licensing.

If road haulage is now free from direct licensing controls, it is far from free from other forms of government control. There are numerous regulations that determine such factors as the weight, size, speed, smoke emission, noise, engine power and state of maintenance of lorries. The 'Construction and Use' regulations also lay down maximum periods for which drivers can be at the wheel of lorries. These regulations, which are aimed at increasing road safety or reducing environmental pollution, can be regarded as a method of adding the social costs on to the private costs of vehicle operation. All these regulations affect the cost of vehicle operation. It would be quite possible for some existing vehicles to carry payloads of about thirty tons instead of the maximum payload now permitted, which is effectively about twenty-two tons. (The maximum legal gross vehicle weight for articulated vehicles is thirty-two tons, and the minimum possible unladen weight that can be achieved is around ten tons.) Since operating costs do not increase in proportion to payloads, the weight restrictions deny operators the enjoyment of potential scale economies. The recent introduction of a minimum power-to-weight ratio of 6 b.h.p. per ton (for all vehicles registered after 1 April 1973) is intended to reduce delay to other road users caused by low-powered lorries A cost–benefit analysis was carried out to estimate the effects of this change and this showed that for a 6 b.h.p. per ton minimum power-to-weight ratio that total benefits would exceed the costs [44]. The main costs resulting from the new regulation will be additions to the operating costs of lorries (through increases in capital costs and fuel costs) and a slight reduction in vehicle payloads. The benefits will come from the increase in the speeds of other road users, and in those of the more powerful lorries themselves. Many other regulations affecting road vehicles have been brought in or changed without the completion of any form of cost–benefit analysis and this means that it is not possible to judge how far they are justified. This is true of the thirty-two-ton gross vehicle weight limit and also of the proposal to reduce maximum driving hours for heavy vehicles from ten to eight hours to conform with E.E.C. regulations. This cut in permitted driving hours would be justified only if there were evidence that it would result in substantial benefits to the community in the reduction of accident rates or in benefits for drivers who preferred the extra leisure to their forgone earnings.

The increasing importance that is being attached to the prevention of environmental pollution means that the main 'growth area' in transport economics is likely to be in the application of cost–benefit analysis to transport problems. The most thorough attempt at using cost–benefit techniques to deal with environmental problems in transport so far carried out has been the work of the Roskill Commission on the site for a third London airport [22]. The discussion on Roskill has focused attention on such issues as time evaluation and the proper ways to measure the costs of noise and other forms of environmental pollution. The Roskill report has been widely criticised [50], but the rejection of its conclusions has been the result of a political value judgement rather than of any clear demonstration that a more perfect cost–benefit analysis of the location decision would have proved that the community will benefit from having an airport sited at Foulness rather than at Cublington. Despite the rejection of the Roskill Commission report, and the resulting scepticism about cost–benefit analysis, it is almost certain that attempts will be made to improve the techniques of analysis and to use them to try to unravel some of the complex transport problems that must be solved. These problems include the development of methods for evaluating urban motorway investment; the whole problem of urban congestion and the use that should be made of city centre areas; the problem of the environmental costs of cars and lorries; the need to measure the benefits gained from the operation of railway passenger services related to the subsidies that should be paid to support them; the desirability of subsidising bus services; the appraisal of port investment; and the development of a proper policy for airport location and the control of supersonic aircraft.

Bibliography

ABBREVIATIONS

E.C.M.T.   European Conference of Ministers of Transport
H.M.S.O.   Her Majesty's Stationery Office
O.E.C.D.   Organisation for Economic Co-operation and Development
R.R.L.   Road Research Laboratory (now Transport and Road Research Laboratory – T.R.R.L.)

REPORTS AND GOVERNMENT PUBLICATIONS

[1] Board of Trade, *British Air Transport in the Seventies* (H.M.S.O., London, 1969).

[2] Board of Trade, *Committee of Inquiry into Shipping – Report* (H.M.S.O., London, May 1970).

[3] British European Airways, *Report and Accounts* (H.M.S.O., London, annual).

[4] British Overseas Airways Corporation, *Report and Accounts* (H.M.S.O., London, annual).

[5] British Railways Board, *Report and Accounts* (financial results and operating statistics) (H.M.S.O., London, annual).

[6] British Road Federation, *Basic Road Statistics* (summary of all statistics relating to road transport and details of recent transport legislation) (B.R.F., London, annual).

[7] British Transport Docks Board, *Report and Accounts* (H.M.S.O., London, annual).

[8] British Waterways Board, *Report and Accounts* (H.M.S.O., London, annual).

[9] General Register Office, *Sample Census 1966, Workplace and Transport Tables* (details of mode of travel to work for people in every local authority area in Britain) (H.M.S.O., London, 1968).

[10] House of Commons, *Sixth Report from the Estimates Committee 1968–69. Motorways and Trunk Roads*, HCP 102–IX (H.M.S.O., London, 1969).

[11] House of Commons, *Select Committee on Nationalised Industries – British Railways* (H.M.S.O., London, 1961).

[12] Ministry of Transport, *Committee of Inquiry into the Major Ports of Great Britain* (Rochdale Committee) (H.M.S.O., London, 1962).

[13] Ministry of Transport (now Department of Environment), *Highways Statistics* (details of passenger and goods vehicles licensed, road traffic, road mileage and expenditure, and estimated ton miles and passenger miles carried) (H.M.S.O., London, annual).

[14] Ministry of Transport (now D.O.E.), *Passenger Transport in Britain* (figures of road, rail and air passenger transport) (H.M.S.O., London, annual).

[15] Ministry of Transport, *Portbury: Reasons for the Minister's decision not to authorise the construction of a new dock at Portbury, Bristol* (H.M.S.O., London, 1966).

[16] Ministry of Transport, *Road Pricing: The Economic and Technical Possibilities* (H.M.S.O., London, 1964).

[17] Ministry of Transport (now D.O.E.), *Roads in England* (details of past and planned road building programme) (H.M.S.O., London, annual).

[18] Ministry of Transport, *Road Track Costs* (H.M.S.O., London, 1968).

[19] Ministry of Transport, *The Transport of Freight* (H.M.S.O., London, 1967).

[20] National Freight Corporation, *Report and Accounts* (includes statistics relating to operation of freightliner trains, former rail parcels services, and British Road Services) (H.M.S.O., London, annual).

[21] National Ports Council, *Report and Accounts* (H.M.S.O., London, annual).

[22] *Report of the Commission on the Third London Airport* (Roskill Report) (H.M.S.O., London, 1971).

BOOKS AND ARTICLES

[23] D. H. Aldcroft, *British Railways in Transition* (Macmillan, London, 1968).

[24] B. Bayliss and J. Hebden, *The Theory and Application of Index Numbers in the Transport Sector* (U.N. Economic Commission for Europe, Geneva, 1971).

[25] G. Becker, 'A Theory of the Allocation of Time', *Economic Journal* (Sep 1965).

[26] M. Beesley, 'Urban Transport – Technical Possibility of Special Taxation in Relation to Congestion Caused by Private Users', *IInd International Symposium on Transport Economics* (E.C.M.T., 1967).

[27] M. Beesley, 'The Value of Time Spent Travelling: some new evidence', *Economica* (May 1965).

[28] M. Beesley and T. C. Evans, *The Costs and Benefits of Road Safety Measures*. E.C.M.T. Ninth Round Table (O.E.C.D., Paris and Washington, 1971).

[29] J. M. Currie, J. A. Murphy and A. Schmitz, 'The Concept of Economic Surplus and its Use in Economic Analysis', *Economic Journal* (Dec 1971).

[30] R. F. F. Dawson, *Cost of Road Accidents in G.B.* (R.R.L. Report LR79, Reading, 1967).

[31] R. F. F. Dawson, *Current Costs of Road Accidents in G.B.* (R.R.L. Report LR396, Reading, 1971).

[32] R. F. F. Dawson, *Estimated Expenditure on Road Transport in G.B. in 1965 and 1966* (R.R.L. Report LR134, Reading, 1967).

[33] R. F. F. Dawson and P. F. Everall, *The Value of Motorists' Time: a Study in Italy* (T.R.R.L. Report LR426, Reading, 1972).

[34] A. DeSerpa, 'A Theory of the Economics of Time', *Economic Journal* (Dec 1971).

[35] Alan W. Evans, 'On the Theory of the Valuations and Allocation of Time', *Scottish Journal of Political Economy* (Feb 1972).

[36] C. B. Foster, *The Transport Problem* (Blackie, Glasgow, 1963).

[37] C. Foster and M. Beesley, 'Estimating the Social Benefits of Constructing an Underground Railway in London', *Journal of the Royal Statistical Society*, series A, part 1 (1963).

[38] C. Foster and M. Beesley, 'The Victoria Line: Social Benefit and Finances', *Journal of the Royal Statistical Society*, series A, part 1 (1965).

78

[39] K. M. Gwilliam, *Transport and Public Policy* (Allen & Unwin, London, 1964).

[40] A. J. Harrison and D. A. Quarmby, *Theoretical and practical research on an estimation of time-saving*. E.C.M.T. Sixth Round Table (O.E.C.D., Paris and Washington, 1969).

[41] A. J. Harrison and S. J. Taylor, 'The Value of Working Time in the Appraisal of Transport Expenditure – A Review', in Dept of the Environment, *Research into the Value of Time,* Time Research Note 16. (This publication also contains other useful discussions of the value of time and a survey of some revealed preference studies.)

[42] C. J. Hawkins and D. W. Pearce, *Capital Investment Appraisal* (Macmillan, London, 1971).

[43] J. R. Hicks, 'The Rehabilitation of Consumers' Surplus', *Review of Economic Studies* (Winter 1940/41).

[44] A. Jennings and C. Sharp, 'More Powerful Engines for Lorries?', *Journal of Transport Economics and Policy* (May 1972).

[45] M. Jones-Lee, 'Valuation of Reduction in Probability of Death by Road Accident', *Journal of Transport Economics and Policy* (Jan 1969).

[46] N. Lee and M. Dalvi, 'Variations in the Value of Travel Time', *Manchester School* (Sep 1969).

[47] Gordon Mills, 'Investment Planning for British Ports', *Journal of Transport Economics and Policy* (May 1971).

[48] R. Millward, *Public Expenditure Economics* (McGraw-Hill, Maidenhead, Berks, 1971).

[49] E. J. Mishan, 'What is Producers' Surplus?', *American Economic Review* (Dec 1968).

[50] E. J. Mishan, 'What is Wrong with Roskill?', *Journal of Transport Economics and Policy* (Sep 1970).

[51] E. Victor Morgan, *Economic and Financial Aspects of Road Improvements* (Roads Campaign Council, London, 1965).

[52] D. L. Munby, 'Mrs. Castle's Transport Policy', *Journal of Transport Economics and Policy* (May 1968).

[53] D. W. Pearce, *Cost–Benefit Analysis* (Macmillan, London, 1971).

[54] A. R. Prest, *Transport Economics in Developing Countries* (Weidenfeld & Nicolson, London, 1969).

[55] R. Pryke, *Public Enterprise in Practice* (MacGibbon & Kee, London, 1971).

[56] D. A. Quarmby, 'Choice of Travel Modes for the Journey to Work', *Journal of Transport Economics and Policy* (Sep 1967).

[57] E. Quinet and H. Schuster, *Pricing the use of infrastructure*, Report of the Seventh Round Table on Transport Economics, E.C.M.T. (O.E.C.D., Paris and Washington, 1971).

[58] P. Redfern, 'Net Investments in Fixed Assets in the U.K., 1938–58', *Journal of the Royal Statistical Society,* series A, (1955), 118.

[59] T. Schelling, 'The Life You Save May Be Your Own', in S. B. Chase, *Problems in Public Expenditure Analysis* (Brookings Instn, London, 1968).

[60] C. H. Sharp, 'Congestion and Welfare – An Examination of the Case for a Congestion Tax', *Economic Journal* (Dec 1966).
and
'Congestion and Welfare – A Reply', *Economic Journal* (June 1969).

[61] C. H. Sharp, *The Problem of Transport* (Pergamon Press, Oxford, 1965).

[62] C. H. Sharp, *Problems of Urban Passenger Transport* (Leicester University Press, 1967).

[63] R. L. Smeed, 'Traffic Studies and Urban Congestion', *Journal of Transport Economics and Policy* (Jan 1968).

[64] D. G. Tipping, 'Time Savings in Transport Studies', *Economic Journal* (Dec 1968).

[65] Sylvia Trench, 'Bus Services in the Nottingham Area', *Journal of Transport Economics and Policy* (May 1971).

[66] W. Vickrey, 'Some Answers to Sharp's Doubts', *Journal of Transport Economics and Policy* (Jan 1968).

[67] A. A. Walters, 'The Long and the Short of Transport', *Bulletin of Oxford Univerity Institute of Economics and Statistics* (May 1965).

[68] A. A. Walters, *The Economics of Road User Charges* (Johns Hopkins U.P., Baltimore, 1968).

[69] D. M. Winch, *Analytical Welfare Economics* (Penguin, Harmondsworth, Middx, 1971).